# ART AND THE WORKING CLASS

# ART AND THE WORKING CLASS

## ALEXANDER BOGDANOV

TRANSLATED AND INTRODUCED BY

### TAYLOR R. GENOVESE

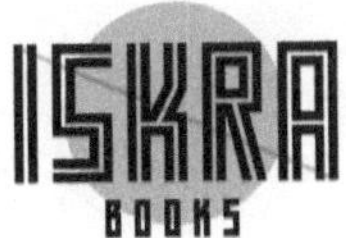

Published by *Iskra Books* 2022

This is an original translation from the monograph *Art and the Working Class* (Искусство и рабочий класс) published by the journal *Proletarian Culture* (Пролетарская Культура) in 1918 at the printing house of I.D. Sytin, Pyatnitskaya Street, Moscow.

All three chapters were first published separately in the journal *Proletarian Culture* in 1918 in Issues 1, 2, and 3 respectively before being compiled into this monograph.

First published in Russian.



**Iskra Books**

U.S. | U.K. | Ireland | Canada | Australia | India

Iskra Books is the imprint of the Center for Communist Studies, an international research center dedicated to the advancement of academic and public scholarship in the field of Marxist-Leninist studies and applied communist theory.

ISBN-13: 978-1-0879-9351-5

**British Library Cataloguing in Publication Data**
A catalogue record for this book is available from the British Library

**Library of Congress Cataloguing-in-Publication Data**
A catalog record for this book is available from the Library of Congress

Typesetting, Art, and Design by Ben Stahnke

Printed and Distributed by IngramSpark

# CONTENTS


Translator's Introduction....................5

1. What is Proletarian Poetry?....................27

2. On Artistic Heritage....................67

3. Critique of Proletarian Art....................101

Bibliography....................137

*The translator wishes to dedicate this to his partner, father, mother, sister, and every working-class artist attempting to bring beauty into a world utterly brutalized by the ugliness of capitalism.*

*And for Alexander Alexandrovich, who truly lived and died for socialism.*

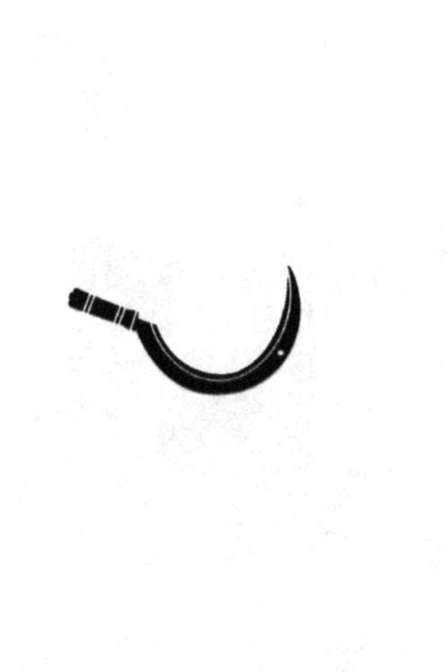

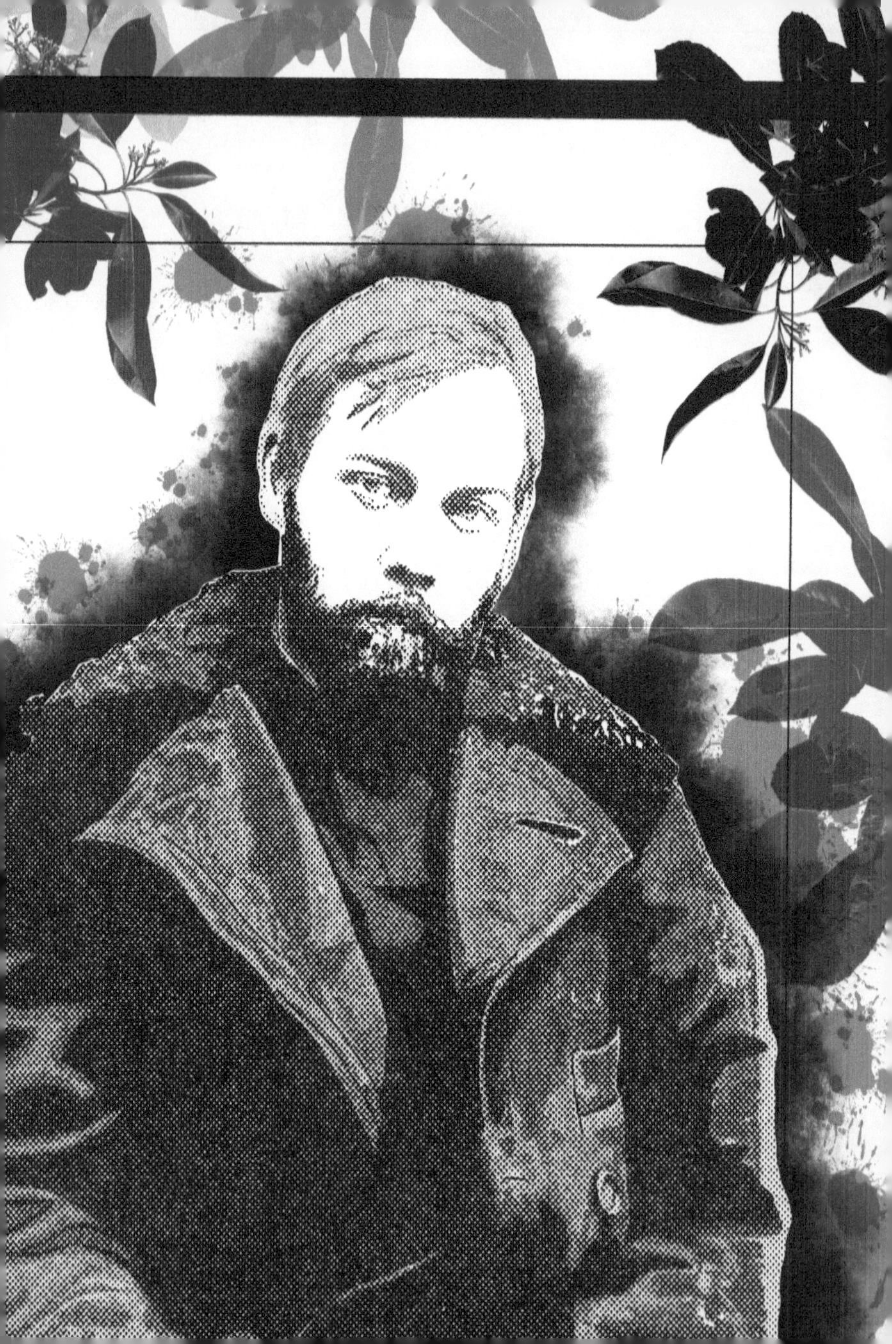

# TRANSLATOR'S INTRODUCTION

Alexander Alexandrovich Malinovsky (1873–1928) was a cultural theorist, science fiction writer, professor, political revolutionary, and economist. Like many revolutionaries, Malinovsky assumed many pseudonyms throughout his life (Verner, Maksimov, Riadovoy), but he eventually settled on adopting his wife's middle name (Bogdanovna) for the majority of his revolutionary, scientific, and cultural career.[1] The son of a member of the local minor gentry and a schoolteacher in Sokolko (a small town in present day Poland), Bogdanov received secondary education in the Russian city of Tula. He then moved on to study the natural sciences as an undergraduate at the University of Moscow before finally earning a graduate degree in psychiatric medicine from the University of Kharkov in 1899.[2] Throughout the 1890s, he was active in the revolutionary underground, leading workers' study circles on economics and Marxism. He was arrested and exiled twice during this period. It was also during this time that he wrote the influential book *A Short Course of Economic Science*, which Vladimir Lenin praised upon its first publication in 1897.[3]

Toward the end of his second exile in 1903, Bogdanov became a supporter of Lenin in his organizational battles against Julius Martov within the Russian Social Democratic Labor Party (RSDLP). In January of 1904, after being freed from exile, Bogdanov immediately traveled to Geneva and attended the founding conference of the Bolshevik faction of the RSDLP (the "Conference of the 22") and was elected to its leadership. He then left for St. Petersburg to support the 1905 Russian Revolution by writing agitprop, publishing tactical leaflets on how to conduct an armed uprising, and editing two Bolshevik-aligned newspapers. As a Bolshevik delegate to the Third Party Congress in 1905, he was elected to the new Central Committee of the RSDLP. In December of 1905, he was arrested—along with the rest of the Executive Committee of the St. Petersburg Soviet of Workers' Deputies—and remained in prison until May of 1906.[4]

It was also during this time that Bogdanov became intensely interested in the philosophy of Richard Avenarius and Ernst Mach. He took their empiricist philosophy of empiriocriticism and attempted to merge it with Marxist historical materialism, calling his transmuted philosophy (and subsequent book) *Empiriomonism*. His ideas were publicly criticized by the Mensheviks as being "idealist," with Georgi Plekhanov being a particularly vocal critic. Lenin also intensely disliked Bogdanov's philosophical positions, but he initially reserved his criticism to private conversations to maintain Bolshevik solidarity and discipline during the revolution.[5] Bogdanov was not discouraged by these negative evaluations, however, and he further refined his ideas of empiriomonism until he developed them into an original philosophy called *tektology*—a forerunner of modern systems theory and cybernetics.[6]

Ultimately, the foremost constants within Bogdanov's life were his attempts at destroying the bourgeois elements embedded within both science and the arts and reconstituting them as proletarian endeavors. To put it bluntly, Bogdanov was exceptionally interested in how to properly wage a cultural revolution. Prior to Antonio Gramsci's articulation of a cultural counter-hegemonic war of position,[7] Bogdanov was similarly worried that without a proper socialist education, the revolutionary masses might unconsciously slip back into bourgeois habits. Beginning in the early 20th century, and accelerating after the 1905 Revolution, Bogdanov, Anatoly Lunacharsky, Maxim Gorky, and others established an organization which they hoped would contribute to a cultural revolution called Proletarian Culture (*Proletarskaya kul'tura*), perhaps more well known by its portmanteau: Proletkult.

Although it is not often framed this way, one can analyze the formation of Proletkult as being forged in the political and ideological battles between Lenin and Bogdanov. In 1909, Bogdanov formed the Bolshevik subfaction *Vpered* (Forward), which promoted the role of the intellectual within the Party, as well as charging itself with developing a strong program for worker education. By prioritizing education, Bogdanov aimed to secure greater roles for the workers within Party leadership. Ironically, this group, which was critical of Lenin, adhered to much of the program Lenin himself had laid out in his seminal work *What Is to Be Done?*[8] In late 1909, *Vpered* organized an experimental proletarian university called The First Higher Social Democratic Propaganda and Agitational School for Workers, housed at Maxim Gorky's home on the Isle of Capri.[9] The establishment of a second Party School soon followed in the Italian city of Bologna between 1910–1911. It was during this time, amid the strengthening hegemony of Bolshevism within the RSDLP, that Lenin and Bogdanov began to publicly accuse each other of deviating from revolutionary Marxism. Lenin was concerned with Bogdanov's "idealism" and Bogdanov with Lenin's "authoritarianism." While each published fair critiques of the other, it is also difficult not to analyze these disputes as at least partially motivated by ego.

Bogdanov was perceived as a threat to Lenin and his followers because he gestured toward a "Bolshevism without Lenin";[10] a Bolshevism that relied on propaganda, ideology, and worker schools rather than one focused on the Party, vanguard, and discipline. Regardless of whomever one sees as politically right or wrong—especially with the clarity of twenty-first century hindsight—it is hard to refute that some of the best political and philosophical work produced by both Bogdanov and Lenin was at least partially due to the dialectical antagonisms between them. In fact, during the crucial time just before and during the 1917 Revolutions, Bogdanov forced Lenin, by way of their philosophical sparring, to clarify and define the contours of what a Bolshevism without Bogdanov would look like—a constellation of ideas that we now call Leninism. As Zenovia Sochor argued, these two men are so philosophically intertwined that it is difficult to grasp some aspects of Leninism without fully comprehending Lenin's disputes with Bogdanov.[11] Indeed, without Bogdanov, there very well may not have been a Leninism—or at least not a Leninism that is as philosophically robust. Thus, it can be argued that Bogdanov and Lenin were the dialectical powerhouses of early Bolshevik thought, not Lenin and Trotsky, as is often teleologically constructed.

Lenin's disdain for what he saw as rising support for "Bogdanovism" (*Bogdanovshchina*) quickly became a political gambit to push Bogdanov out of Party leadership, culminating in his eventual expulsion from the Party itself. This worry was not entirely without justification; Bogdanovism seemed to be the second most popular ideology among the cohort of 1917 revolutionaries, just after Leninism.[12] Two of Lenin's closest associates—Maxim Gorky and Nikolai Bukharin—were influenced by, and publicly defended, Bogdanov's ideas on proletarian culture. The Scientific Organization of Labor (*Nauchnaya organizatsiya truda*, or NOT), which was enthusiastically praised by Lenin, was led by two early members of Proletkult: Platon Kerzhentsev and Aleksei Gastev—the latter of whom is quoted extensively throughout this book. Even Lenin's pet project—the State Commission for the Electrification of Russia (**Go***sudarstvennaya komissiya po* **e***lektrifikatsii* **Ro***ssii*, or GOELRO)—the venture which led to one of Lenin's most famous quotes, "Communism is Soviet power plus electrification of the whole country,"[13] was realized by followers of Bogdanov, among them economists Vladimir Bazarov and Vladimir Groman.[14]

But according to interviews with Bogdanov's son, the rivalry between Lenin and Bogdanov has been misunderstood by many historians. His son has claimed that the enmity between these two men was largely philosophical (and personal) in nature, rather than one based on perceived political ambitions from Bogdanov to "take over" the Party.[15] Bogdanov was not interested in chasing political clout—he was only interested in establishing political structures that would help strengthen the socialist revolution, which he saw as already rolling ahead on its own accord. In fact, by 1918, Bogdanov took to describing himself as "a nonparty socialist, a scientific and cultural worker."[16] This is hardly the way someone hoping to take control of a revolutionary party would describe themselves. Bogdanov's disinterest in usurping Lenin seems to be confirmed by leading Bolshevik figures such as Mikhail Pokrovsky, Nikolai Bukharin, and Joseph Stalin, all of whom urged Bogdanov to rejoin the Party and assume a leadership position after Lenin's death, a gesture that certainly would not have been extended to a political rival.[17]

This comradely relationship with Communist Party leadership should not be particularly shocking. If one really digs into the writings of Bogdanov and Lenin, one can see that the two were largely in agreement with one another—their differences were minor and centered almost exclusively on revolutionary strategy. Yet political propagandizing during the Cold War years have led some to uphold Bogdanov as some kind of anti-Leninist hero—an anti-authoritarian figure who could then be framed as a victim of Soviet power within the imaginations of anti-authoritarian leftists and Western Cold Warriors alike.[18] But, in fact, Bogdanov was skeptical (and sometimes outright hostile) to the ideas of libertarian socialism. For example, he agreed with Leninist critiques of syndicalism and worker control of unions, calling anarcho-syndicalism "[individualism] from the left" and trade-unionism "[individualism] from the right."[19] In his science fiction novels, including his most famous work *Red Star* (*Krasnaya zvezda*), Bogdanov envisioned the future of communism as being highly centralized, with labor being managed and assigned by a central labor organization that had very little direct input from the workers.[20] Yet Bogdanov was a proper dialectician. In his *A Short Course of Economic Science*, he contended that worker class consciousness could develop spontaneously, and he also encouraged workers to actively participate in trade unions. His critiques of these organizations stemmed from a materialist analysis that trade unions and other worker-organized groups often operated solely within the logics of capital and tended to act as collections of individuals rather than collectives—arguably a problem we still face today.[21] Additionally, it is worth pointing out that Bogdanov's commentary differs little from Marx and Engels' own position in *The Communist Manifesto*. Far from an anarchist or syndicalist, Bogdanov's positions might be considered closer to the left-communists (although he quarreled quite a bit with them as well).

Furthermore, although the subjects of culture and art were often intense points of conflict between Bogdanov and Lenin, here too they tended to agree on a great many points, battling mainly over strategic ways forward. One of the biggest cultural challenges the revolution faced was how to reconcile socialist aesthetic development with past artistic achievements produced under a bourgeois hegemony. Lenin himself complained that many Marxist theorists refused to confront this problem; that there would be a "concrete, practical difficulty that would confront the working class when it took power, when it set itself the task of turning the sum total of the very rich, historically inevitable, and necessary for us, store of culture and knowledge and technique accumulated by capitalism [and transform it] from an instrument of capitalism into an instrument of socialism."[22] I will refrain from extensively quoting Bogdanov's positions because he devotes the entirety of Chapter 2 to this problem, but the two men both agreed that it was necessary to utilize a "critical assimilation" of past artistic achievements, rather than the outright destruction of them. Their philosophical clashing came down to strategy—Lenin prioritized assimilation whereas Bogdanov stressed criticism.[23] But both men found it highly distressing that younger generations of artists were beginning to outright reject the art of the past. For example, Lenin said "Why turn our backs on what is truly beautiful, abandon it as the point of departure for further development solely because it is 'old'?"[24] Lenin much preferred Pushkin to contemporary artists like Mayakovsky and was taken aback when students vehemently rejected the former because he was "bourgeois."[25] Bogdanov shared Lenin's feelings. In Chapter 3, Bogdanov writes: "It is distressing to see when a poet-proletarian is looking for the best artistic forms and they think they will find them in some show-off intellectual advertiser like Mayakovsky." In the same chapter, he argues that "the poet does not have the right to disrespect the great dead who paved the way for us and who bequeathed their souls to us—who, from the grave, extend a helping hand to us in our pursuit of the ideal."

But where Lenin saw cultural revolution as a series of stages that operated through dialectical processes of assimilation and incorporation, Bogdanov saw it as consisting of indeterminate catalysts. He stressed that if the proletariat was not prepared with the intellectual tools of ruthless critique, the revolution could regress due to a lingering of bourgeois culture and ideology. This "cultural lag" needed to be combatted through persistent political education programs that would completely transform society, severing the bourgeois "ideological remnants" that acted as "intermediary links" between the base and superstructure.[26] Therefore, for Bogdanov, revolution was waged on a continuum, with a seizure of state power happening after, or in tandem with, the establishment of a new cultural hegemony. Or, as he put it: "Socialist development will be crowned with a socialist revolution" (*Sotsialisticheskoye razvitiye zavershitsya sotsialisticheskoy revolyutsiyey*).[27] Educational and cultural tasks needed to become primary responsibilities for the revolution, not ancillary ones. This also meant that Bogdanov viewed militancy and violence as foreign to proletarian culture. While he understood that struggle was essential (and he himself participated in violent revolutionary activity), he believed that "proletarian culture is basically defined not by struggle, but by labor, not by destruction, but by creativity" (*Proletarskaya kul'tura opredelyayetsya v osnove ne bor'boy, a trudom, ne razrusheniyem, a tvorchestvom*).[28] As he discusses in this book, Bogdanov was disturbed by the increasing prevalence of military culture within the revolution, and, for that matter, with what he saw as a developing militant dogmatism of Marxist ideology itself.

These positions naturally led many to brand Bogdanov as a revisionist and an idealist. But Bogdanov understood Marxism as being a "teaching that radically denies all absolute and eternal truths" and that it should be the starting point of analysis, not its definitive end.[29] He was concerned with what he saw as a tendency for both leading revolutionaries and ordinary workers to approach Marxist texts as the "Holy Scriptures of Marx and Engels" (*Svyashchennomu Pisaniyu Marksa i Engel'sa*).[30] Bogdanov urged fellow revolutionaries not to allow the theories of Marx and others to ossify into some kind of an eternal truth—the idea of eternal truths being nothing but an example of a fetish to Bogdanov —because social conceptions of "truth" were always contingent upon material conditions, cultural values, and other historical variables.[31] As a Marxist, Bogdanov understood the relationship between being and consciousness, structures and values. His proposals to focus less on party discipline and more on "comradely relations" and collectivism was motivated by a desire to develop cultural structures that might alter the existing values molded by capitalism, reconstituting them into sets of values more in line with socialism. Bogdanov was ahead of his time in that he wished to add cultural criteria to Marx's economic ones, especially when it came to the definition of classes. He agreed that worker ownership of the means of production was necessary, but focusing solely on political economy would be insufficient for producing a classless society. In other words, material conditions alone were not enough; without a cultural revolution, people would remain divided due to layers of cultural and psychological differences. Without a counter-hegemonic cultural program, the working class would be vulnerable to outdated, yet stubbornly embedded, norms and attitudes, leading to feelings of alienation—perhaps without even understanding why. Essentially, what Bogdanov saw himself doing was making explicit what was already implicit within Marxism and proposing programs that might curb the imperfections that naturally occur in spontaneous revolutionary developments.[32] Bogdanov argued that "proletarian culture is the socialist ideal in its development" (*Proletarskaya kul'tura yest' sotsialisticheskiy ideal v yego razvitii*)[33] and that the socialist ideal must contain both "political *and* cultural liberation."[34] *Art and the Working Class* was written to further these positions.

By 1920, Bogdanov's perceived revisionism and his quarrels with Lenin came to a boiling point. Lenin published a new edition of his book *Materialism and Empirio-criticism*, which was a pointed critique of

Bogdanov's theories of empiriomonism and *tektology*. Lenin also launched an offensive against Proletkult, eventually subsuming the organization into the state-run People's Commissariat for Education (***Narodnyy komissariat prosveshcheniya***, or Narkompros). The early 1920s were a time of near-constant media attacks on Bogdanov, even as he attempted to retreat out of political life and into the academy. Bogdanov was arrested in September 1923 under suspicion of supporting an opposition group called Workers' Truth (*Rabochaya pravda*). After his arrest, he requested to be interrogated by his old colleague and head of the State Political Directorate (*Gosudarstvennoe politicheskoe upravlenie*, or GPU) Felix Dzerzhinsky. Bogdanov was able to convince Dzerzhinsky that not only was he not a member of Workers' Truth, he also did not believe the positions that he was accused of believing—mainly that the New Economic Policy was an occluded program of advanced capitalism. In October of 1923, he was released from prison, but outlets willing to publish his political and cultural writing began to narrow. Most of his last works appear only in the university journal of the Communist Academy, where he was a professor.[35]

After resigning from Proletkult and with almost no outlets willing to publish his writing, Bogdanov turned to his last remaining passion: medicine. He was primarily interested in experimenting with what he had only written about in his science fiction novels: "mutual" (*vzaimnye*) blood exchanges between the young and the old that might be therapeutically and holistically rejuvenative—or as he described them in *Red Star*, "comradely exchanges of life [that] extend beyond the ideological dimension into the physiological one."[36] This attracted the attention of his former colleagues in the upper strata of the Soviet state, many of whom were suffering from an endemic of poor health (and even sudden death) from what Party doctors described as revolutionary "fatigue" (*iznoshennost'* or *utomleniye*) and which eventually became known as "Soviet exhaustion."[37] After hearing about early European successes in curing "exhaustion" with blood rejuvenation, Stalin appointed Bogdanov the Founding Director of the Institute for Hematology and Blood Transfusions in 1926, the first such institute not only in the Soviet Union, but also the world.[38] Bogdanov tested his theories largely on himself—participating eleven times in experimental blood transfusions and exchanges by the beginning of 1928—and noted that, following multiple treatments, his eyesight improved, his balding suspended, and friends commented that he looked and acted ten years younger.

In the spring of 1928, Bogdanov decided to exchange blood with a student who was suffering from malaria and tuberculosis in an attempt to assist with their affliction. Although the student ended up making a full recovery after the exchange, Bogdanov suffered a hemolytic transfusion reaction. Two weeks later he was dead at the age of 54.

Within the past 15 years, there has been a resurgence of interest in Alexander Bogdanov and his ideas. Unfortunately, his scientific achievements seem to have been hijacked by capital. The possible benefits of blood exchanges have been appropriated by several Silicon Valley and European tech companies—but instead of Bogdanov's "comradely exchange," they have opted to focus on bringing the *capitalist* ideology into the physiological by charging between \$8,000–\$12,000 for "young blood infusions."[39] Within more revolutionary spheres, the importance of culture and art is being taken more seriously. Yet here too the forces of reaction and chauvinism, including on the left, have commandeered the conversation. Discourse around so-called "patriotic socialism" and "cancel culture" have sadly vindicated Bogdanov's dire warnings—without a cultural revolution, even well-meaning comrades will inevitably reproduce oppressive regimes of thought and subsequently damage our march toward communism.

Throughout Bogdanov's corpus of writing, he

often references Shakespeare's *Hamlet* (with this book being no exception). Bogdanov saw Hamlet as a character who, being a formidable descendant of the Vikings, was born into the art of warfare, but whose natural proclivities skewed toward culture and the arts.[40] Perhaps he was drawn to Hamlet because he saw this similar dichotomy within himself. As twenty-first century communists, I think many of us can relate to this feeling. And indeed, our world necessitates that we must cultivate within ourselves both the fighter and the aesthete. Or, as Bogdanov says in Chapter 2, we must each become "an active aesthete, a fighter for the harmony of life." The only way forward in our distressing reality of intensified ecological, social, and economic disaster is through intensive study with holistic thinkers like Bogdanov, followed by the material enactment of our expertise through praxis. And it is for this reason that I humbly offer this original English translation of his previously untranslated pamphlet *Art and the Working Class.*

•

*A brief comment on structure*: all endnotes are translator's notes meant to assist the reader in contextualizing and understanding certain words, phrases, people, places, and things referenced by Bogdanov. Every citation that Bogdanov made in his manuscript has remained in-text to uphold the fidelity of the original document.

*By way of acknowledgements*: I would like to thank all my comrades at the Center for Communist Studies and Iskra Books for their encouragement, solidarity, and labor reviewing drafts; and in particular, I'd like to thank Ben Stahnke, who was my editor, and who also illustrated and designed the amazing cover and chapter artwork, and Christian Noakes, who reviewed several drafts and provided invaluable comments. I'd also like to thank my parents, Ginnie and Bob, for their constant love and support. One of the main reasons I'm so interested in Bogdanov and Proletkult is because my acting teacher, Robert Encila, took a chance on me as an inexperienced actor in 2005 and cast me in the show *America Hurrah*, which opened my eyes to the revolutionary potential of art and theatre—thank you. Thanks also to the Alexander Bogdanov Library, part of the Historical Materialism series at Brill, for providing a wealth of original scans of Bogdanov's writing. And last, but definitely not least, thanks to my partner Amber and our dog Murphy for tolerating the many late nights of my staring at hundred-year-old scans of Russian political pamphlets. I couldn't do any of this without you.

TRG 2021

## NOTES

1. Bogdanov 2016, pp. vii.

2. *Ibid*, pp. ix; White 2019, pp. 1.

3. Bogdanov 2016, pp. ix.

4. *Ibid.* pp. x.

5. *Ibid.* However, as the Bolsheviks became more secure within the RSDLP, Lenin could no longer keep quiet about his disdain for Bogdanov's philosophical and political positions and, in 1909, he published his take-down piece of Bogdanov's philosophy entitled *Materialism and Empirio-criticism*, which initiated Bogdanov's eventual expulsion from the Party.

6. Sochor 1988, pp. 55.

7. Gramsci 1971.

8. Lenin 1960.

9. Scherrer 1998.

10. Williams 1980, pp. 401.

11. Sochor 1988, pp. 175.

12. Sochor 1988, pp. 13; Utechin 1958, pp. 115.

13. Lenin 1966, pp. 419.

14. Sochor 1988, pp. 12.

15. Ibid., pp. 13.

16. Bogdanov 1918a.

17. Sochor 1988, pp. 13.

18. See Williams 1980.

19. Bogdanov 1911, pp. 48.

20. Bogdanov 1984.

21. Bogdanov 1918b.

22. Lenin 1965, pp. 412.

23. Sochor 1988, pp. 182.

24. Zetkin 1956, pp. 19.

25. Sochor 1988, pp. 172.

26. Bogdanov 1906.

27. Bogdanov 1918b, pp. 102.

28. Bogdanov 1920, pp. 91.

29. Bogdanov 1911.

30. Bogdanov 1918b, pp. 61.

31. Suchor 1988, pp. 187.

32. *Ibid.*, pp. 34–35.

33. Bogdanov 1920, pp. 91.

34. Suchor 1988, pp. 185; emphasis added.

35. White 2019.

36. Bogdanov 1984, pp. 86.

37. Jarovsky 1989; Krementsov 2011; Zalkind 1925.

38. Krementsov 2011; White 2019.

39. Genovese 2019.

40. White 2019.

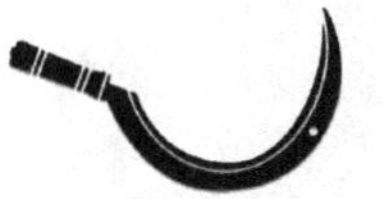

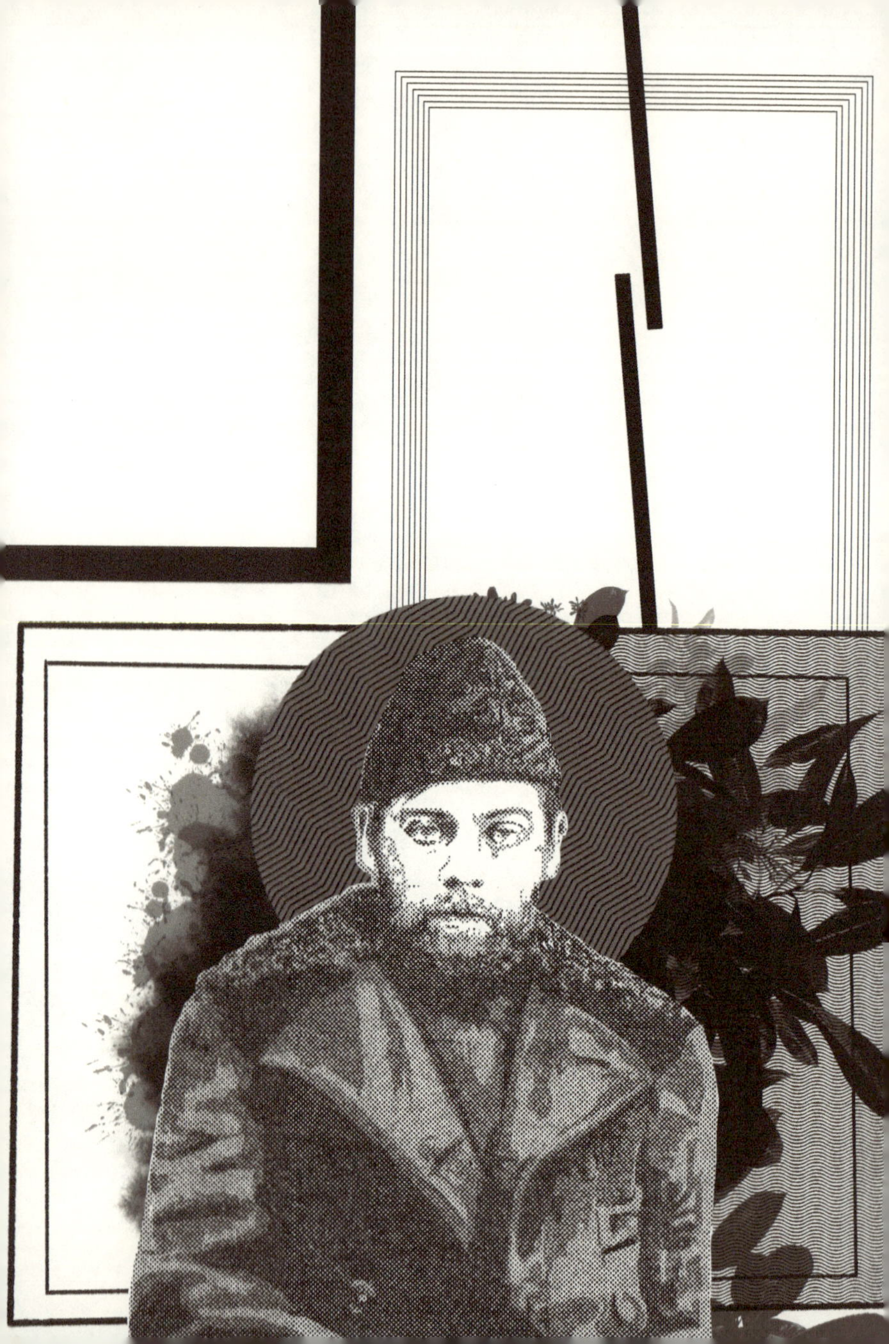

1

# WHAT IS PROLETARIAN POETRY?

## I.

Proletarian poetry is, first of all, *poetry*, a specific form of *art*.

There is no poetry, nor any art in general, without *living images*. If the multiplication tables or the laws of physics were somehow recited in smooth and finished poetic verse, this would still not be poetry, because abstract concepts are not living images.

There is also no poetry, nor any art in general, without *harmony* in the combination of images—without any connection or link between them, without what might be called "organization." If, for example, illustrated figures are not linked with one another in a united plan, or if they are placed randomly and without order, then this is not a picture; this is not a painting.

A few months ago, a newspaper published poetry

that began like this:

> "War until victory, war without end!"
> The merchant's pockets scream with ecstasy;
> He does not care about the blood of those lost,
> Only after a profit will the war end.
> The industrialist, too, filled his pockets,
> Deliberately deceiving the workers!
> ...etc.

It was a crime on the part of the editorial board to publish such verses: a crime against the reader, and a crime against the author—an ordinary, sincere, and honest worker, who simply did not know what poetry is. Here, either there are no living images at all ("only after a profit will the war end," "the industrialist deliberately deceives the workers"), or the images are in sharp contradiction with one another (pockets both "scream" and are filled with "ecstasy"). It is as if we have deliberately written an example of something contrary to the essence of art.

One must know and remember this: art is the organization of living images and poetry is the organization of living images in verbal form.

## II.

The origin of poetry is the same as that of human discourse in general.

The spontaneous cries that escaped from primitive humanity during the stresses of their work—their *cries of labor*—were the embryos of words, the first means of designating something, starting with the actions that provoked these cries. This vocal medium was natural and understandable to all who could hear it. These same labor cries were also the genesis of the *labor song.*

The labor song was not just sung for fun or entertainment. Through common labor, these songs united the efforts of the workers, giving their actions harmony, cadence, and cohesion. It was, therefore, a *means of organizing collective action.* It retains this value even now.

In a battle song, which developed later, the organizational meaning is more nuanced. This type of song was usually sung *before* the battle, and created a sentiment of solidarity, *a bond of collective feeling*—the fundamental condition for a united and coordinated combat action. This is, so to speak, the preliminary mode of organizing, particularly for such difficult tasks that await any collective force.

The second root of poetry is myth; in general, this

is also the beginning of *knowledge*.

Originally, words denoted human action. It was with these words alone that people could communicate with each other about the events and actions of nature and its elemental forces. Thus, even in the simplest story or description, nature inevitably became personified. Whether we were talking about an animal, a tree, the sun or the moon, a river or a stream, it was as if everything we were talking about were a person: the sun "goes" across the sky, in the morning it "rises," in the evening it "sets," in winter it is "sick," it is "losing weight," and in the spring it is "recovering," etc. This involuntary transfer of concepts from the human to the elemental is called "the basic metaphor." Without it, human thought would not have been able to do work upon the extra-human world around it—we would not have developed knowledge.

Later, little by little, human thought assimilated the difference between thinking and human externalities— it freed itself from the basic metaphor, especially after having developed the names for *things*. But in essence, even now, it is still far from being completely free from this metaphor. Even the very word "*mir*"[1] is itself one of these remnants, because it means, properly speaking, a community, a collective of people. And in poetry, the role of the basic metaphor has always been, and still remains, enormous. The personification of nature is a poetic process.

Initially, early myths contained no fiction. When a father would pass on to his children what he himself knew from his experience of, for example, the varying fate of the sun in its annual cycle, this lecture in primitive astronomy inevitably took the form of a story about the adventures of a good and powerful man and his struggle against enemy forces that either fled before him or inflicted defeats and wounds upon him, sapping him of his strength, etc. From there, poetic myths began to develop further: among the Babylonians there was the hero Gilgamesh and among the Greeks there was Hercules. Further afield, when an experienced person would teach a less experienced person that dead bodies were unhealthy for the living to be around—that they caused disease and even death—then a story would arise describing the evil dead, about their enmity toward the living, from which the myth of vampires and ghouls was later formed. During this time, myths were the only possible way to transmit *knowledge* in a society.

Poetry, prose, science—all of these were inseparably fused within the indeterminate embryo that was primitive myth. But the concrete meaning of these myths—its meaning for society—is quite precise. In fact, it has, once again, become an instrument for transforming the social and working lives of people.

Why is the knowledge of peoples—about themselves, life, and nature—collected and passed on for generation upon generation? It is to take account of this knowledge, to lead and unite—in general, to *organize* the practical efforts of people *on the basis of this knowledge*. The initial solar myth—the description of the changing of the seasons—guided the cycle of not just agricultural work, but also hunting, fishing, and every activity whose organization was based on a seasonal distribution of labor, on a "temporal orientation." The myths surrounding the dead led to hygiene measures concerning corpses—for example, one must bury them at a sufficient depth, away from homes, etc. Primitive, poetic knowledge assisted in the organization of time-based practices in the same way that our more recent exact sciences assist in organizing contemporary production.

## III.

Has the vital meaning of poetry essentially changed since then?

Let us remember what the poetry of Homer and Hesiod were for the ancient Greeks: the most important means of education. And what is education?

It is the basic organizational mode that brings new members into a society.

A human child is reared and nurtured in order to become a useful and living link within a system of social relations, in order to take their place and fulfill their tasks within general social processes. Education organizes the human collective in the same way that order, discipline, and combat techniques organize an army.

Our theorists, in keeping with the aristocratic and partly bourgeois tradition—who regard art as an "ornament of life," as a kind of luxury—do not understand to what degree they contradict themselves when, at the same time, they recognize that art holds an educational meaning; that is to say, a practical and organizational meaning.

There are two of these bourgeois theories: "pure art" and "civic art." The first asserts that art *must* be an end in itself, *must* be free from the interests and aspirations of the practical struggles of humanity. The second believes that art *must* bring the progressive tendencies of this struggle into a person's life. We must reject both of these theories. First, let us look at what art actually *is* in the life of humankind. It organizes its forces in complete independence from any civic tasks that may or may not be imposed upon it. There is no need to force these tasks upon art—this would be an inconvenience for the artist and unnecessarily harmful to the quality of their art. The artist can organize living images much more harmoniously when they are able to do so freely, without constraints or instructions. But it is also absurd to forbid art from having political and socially combative motives. Its content is the *whole* of life, without limits or prohibitions.

The most "pure" area of poetry is lyrical poetry—the art of personal states of mind, of emotions, of feeling. But who and what is this poetry able to socially organize?

If lyrical poetry only expressed the personal emotions of the poet, then it would not be understandable or interesting to anyone else—it would not be art. Its meaning lies in its ability to reproduce a common state of mind in a highly diverse group of people, yet a group of people whose souls are similar to one another. By revealing and making intelligible to people this common thread, the poet unites them in an indivisible way—the poet welds them together through a unity of affective mutual understanding, through a "sympathy" which is provoked in all of them. And, at the same time, the poet *educates* this part of the peoples' soul to point them all in the same direction, which widens and deepens their intimacy, reinforcing the solidity of their social and class bonds. This prepares and develops the possibility of concerted, coordinated actions among the people. As in the battle song above, it becomes a matter of organizing a peoples' collective forces and directing them toward serving their common way of life, their common struggle.

And this poetry—which describes life as an epic, a drama, a novel—is, in its organizational meaning, similar to science. It serves to guide, on the basis of past experience, the arrangement of mutual relations between people. Thus, epic poems give living examples of mass action: examples of the link between the "heroes"—or "leaders"—and the "crowd" that marches behind them, examples of the way collective forces of the world struggle and reconcile, etc. The majority of novels, especially at their most romantic, give a variety of concrete examples to similar problems: how men and women, starting as individuals placed in different conditions, form basic social organizations in the form of a family; then how different individuals, such as relatives, adapt to the new social environment forming around them. Dramatic action exposes organizational conflicts and their resolutions. In our time, at least for the urban population, poetry (and fiction in general) are perhaps the most widespread and significant means of education—that is, devices for explaining how a person is introduced into a system of social connections.

## IV.

Contemporary society is divided into *classes*. They are communities divided by many concrete contradictions and therefore, they are organized separately, in dissimilar ways, one *against* the other. Of course, their organizational tools—that is, their ideologies—are also different and distinct. In many cases, not only do they not have anything in common, but they are directly incompatible with each other. This also applies to poetry. Within a class society, there also exists class poetry: landlord, peasant, bourgeois, and proletarian.

Of course, this should not be understood in the sense that *poetry defends the interests* of this or that class, although this is sometimes the case, especially in political and civic poetry, but this is relatively rare. In general, its class character lies much deeper. It consists of the fact that a poet *stands in the position* of a determined class: they see the world through the eyes of their class, they think and feel things according to the social nature of their class. Under the author-individual lies both the author-collective and the author-class. Poetry, then, becomes part of their self-awareness and identity.

The author-individual may not think about it at all; they may not even suspect it. The works themselves often contain no direct indication, nor any mention, of their class origin. Take, for example, the lyrical poetry of Fet.[2] In his beautiful poetry, the manifestations of living nature are elegantly rendered into words that have been generated by a refined soul. His poetry, at first glance, seems to be an example of "pure art," devoid of any political or social ulterior motives. However, even before the introduction of Marxism in Russia, there were people who knew immediately that this was *"barskaya"*[3] poetry. People were able to recognize Fet's work as *"barskaya,"* that is, poetry for stately landowners, generated by the moods, situations, and forms of existence within the landowning classes of our country. This is the truth of the matter.

Fet's poetry radiates a deep and total detachment from everyday material and economic concerns—a reality that was only possible for the noble, landlord elements of society, who were increasingly becoming more detached from production. The bourgeoisie itself, then in full swing, was preoccupied with profit and competition—saturated in a business-like atmosphere—and could not cultivate refined sensations and feelings. And aside from that, the bourgeoisie were essentially urban, and therefore they were incapable of perceiving nature as finely as the landlords in the countryside. On the other hand, it is not difficult to see that this poetry was, in reality, an organizing force for the landlord class—a class that was already outdated but, of course, fiercely defended its interests, as it did not want to leave the historical stage. Such poetry not only united the representatives of the nobility through a kind of collective sentiment, but it also indirectly placed the nobles in opposition with the rest of society, thereby strengthening their class cohesion. This poetry reinforced the belief in their natural superiority and privileged place above society; it was as if they were saying "what sublime and tasteful beings *we* are, how gentle and refined are *our* souls, this is how noble *our* culture is." And from there, their ambition spontaneously arose to defend their culture both firmly and unanimously—that is to say (obviously), they were dead-set on defending the essential conditions of their class: their material wealth and their dominating social positions.

In a class society, poetry *cannot be situated outside of class*; but this also does not mean that it belongs, in each given case, to one particular class. Nekrasov's[4] poetry, for example, contains at once clear remnants of the psychology of the landlord class in which he was raised, as well as the constraints of the urban intelligentsia who consumed his work. But it also contains fiery defenses and vivid expressions of the aspirations, thoughts, and feelings of the peasant classes for whom he felt a deep compassion for. This is *mixed-class* poetry. In our time, this is the most prominent form of poetry, a kind of democratic poetry: peasant-intellectuals, worker-peasants, worker-peasant-intellectuals. It would be easy to classify many of our more recent popular poets in this way.

The proletariat does not, of course, need such poetry—they need pure class poetry: *proletarian* poetry.

## V.

The character of proletarian poetry is defined by the existential and fundamental conditions of the working class itself: its position in production, its type of organization, and its historical destiny.

The proletariat is a working, exploited, struggling, and progressive class. It is a class that is concentrated predominantly in cities, and they are characterized by a *comradely form of cooperation*. All these characteristics are inevitably reflected in their collective consciousness—in their ideology—and therefore, in their poetry. But even if these features do not always *characterize* proletarian poetry, they do distinguish it from other types.

Does work—that is, exploitation by the ruling

classes, the struggle against their oppression, and the aspirations for progress—differentiate the proletariat from the poorest peasantry or from the lowest strata of the working intelligentsia? Obviously not. These features are also present in the non-proletariat groups, and because of that, it brings them closer to the working class. However, these other groups were able to create their poetry earlier than the proletariat; the latter joined them much later on the path toward poetic creation. Because of this, the proletariat's early attempts at art have an *indefinite class character*: that of revolutionary-democratic poetry. Here, for example, is a beautiful song, written by a young worker, Alexey Gmyrev,[5] who died in prison several years ago.

### SCARLET

We are going towards the sun. We are going,
And toward freedom we sing a scarlet song.

Scarlet rings over the land, it buzzes,
Awakening, terrifying, like war.

Calling on those who, in their heart and soul, are proud,
Our song pours powerfully over the ground.

We go towards the Sun, we go
And we carry the scarlet banner of freedom.

We painted our banner with the blood of the Sun,
And it burns, conquering the prophetic darkness.

The crêpe of those who have fallen is a black flagpole.
It is good to carry our banner and it is easy.

We walk under the scarlet banner, we walk
With a scarlet song, on a sunny, scarlet path.

Our path is long, eternal, age-old;
But it is the purest and most direct.

We are few, we are few; but on the way
Millions of fighters will join us

To carry our burden, our banner, freedom, blood!
We are crazy, but like immortal love.

So no crying and no resting at the graves.
Further, further, all who love the Sun!

We go towards the Sun, we go
And we sing, and we carry the scarlet banner.

Here, besides the background of the author, there is nothing that would make this song a truly *proletarian* song. Along with the workers, it could have inspired, and united in revolutionary momentum, both the former militants of the advanced intelligentsia—that is to say, those of People's Will[6]—as well as the peasant fighters of Land and Freedom.[7] Thus, much of the old revolutionary poetry was a product of several circles: the intelligentsia, the peasantry, and the working class.

## VI.

What essentially differentiates the proletariat from other democratic elements is its particular type of work and cooperation.

The most profound break in the working nature of humanity was when one's "brain" separated from their "working hands"—the detachment of "direction" from "execution"—when one began to think, decide, and command others to carry out specific orders. This became the separation of the *organizer* from the *performer*; it was the origin of power—which is to say, the origin of submission. One person in relation to another became a *superior being*, and with that, a sense of *admiration* arose. On this basis, a religious worldview began to develop. Prior to this, such a conception could not exist because nature—the elements and their terrifying forces—aroused in humanity an animal-like fear, rather than a "fear of God." Nature's forces produced in humankind a fear of powerful natural enemies instead of thoughts about qualitatively superior beings who had the ability to stir feelings of both humility and admiration—without the latter, there could be no religion. Authoritarian collaboration, as it grew and deepened, imbued human consciousness with a sense of authority: all of nature was to be subordinated by those who govern and organize—that is to say, by deities. Now everyone was given a manager—a soul.

By the very nature of their work, the organizer is indeed of a qualitatively superior kind, and the performer is of an inferior kind. In one, there is initiative, consideration, observation, and control; at the same time, there is also a requirement for experience, knowledge, and intense attention. In the other, none of these are required. The latter only needs passive discipline and blind obedience in order to mechanically carry out their work. It is useless for the slave, the serf, the soldier of some ancient despot to think while doing a job—and it can even be harmful. They are living tools, nothing more.

The other break in the working nature of humanity is *specialization*. Each specialist has their own task, their own experience, their own special little world. The farmer knows their field, their plow, their horse; the blacksmith knows their forge, their bellows, their hammers; the shoemaker knows their skins, their awls, their shoe trees. None of them can know—nor, consequently, want to know—the work of the other. It is better to concentrate on their own work and perfect their craft. However, this break, this rupture, is further deepened by the isolation and independence of these specialized economies, which only meet on the market when it is time to exchange their products. There, any existing reciprocal relations completely disappear under the struggle of all against all: buyers against sellers for the price, sellers amongst themselves for sales, and buyers amongst themselves for obtaining a desired product that is scarce.

This second break in the nature of work gave rise to *individualism*. Humankind has taken the habit of perceiving and thinking of themselves as being in opposition to others. They see themselves as a fundamentally separate creature, with fundamentally separate interests; from their aspirations to their actions, they are an individual distinct from their social environment. For them, the individual—this autonomous "me"—is the center of their perception and understanding of the world. The freedom of this "me" is the highest ideal.

These two ruptures in the nature of work pass through the consciousness of the old classes, which means that they also pass through their poetry. The poetry and myths of a purely authoritarian era, such as feudalism, is imbued through and through with the spirit of authoritarianism—for example, the Book of Genesis among the Jews, "The Iliad" and "The Odyssey" among the Greeks, the "Mahābhārata" among the Hindus, the *byliny*[8] and "The Tale of Igor's

Campaign"[9] among the Russians. These myths and poems reduce the entire course of life—its chain of events—to the activities of gods, heroes, kings, and leaders. Their lyrics—a vivid example being the Psalms by David—treat nature as a manifestation of divine will, imbued with prayer and humility. In the poetry of the bourgeois world, individualism reigns supreme: at the center is their personality, their destinies, their experiences; poems, novels, and dramas all depict their collisions with the outside world, their relationship to other people and to nature, their struggle for happiness or career, their creativity, victories, and defeats. The lyrics all boil down to individual psychology, to the emotional movements and moods of an individual: their subjective feelings about nature, their joys, sadness, dreams, disappointments, and sexual love— with its suffering and delight. Such is the content of their lyrics.

It should be noted that the poetry of the bourgeois world retains many remnants of authoritarian consciousness because bourgeois society retains many elements of authoritarian collaboration, of power— that is to say, submission. In addition, the diversity of bourgeois groups—the big and small capitalists, the upper intelligentsia, both the backward and progressive landowners, the stock market speculators, the rentiers, not to mention the mixtures and crossovers between these groups—naturally gives rise to a variety of forms and content within their poetry, although the fundamental genre remains the same.

### VII.

In mechanized production, for the first time, the fundamental ruptures that exist in the nature of work have begun to fuse together. In this mode of production, the "worker's hand" is not simply a hand—and the worker is not simply a passive, mechanical performer. They are submissive, but they *control* the "iron slave," the machine. The more complex the machine, the more their labor is reduced to observation and control—to understanding all the aspects and settings of the operation of the machine—and intervention by the worker is only needed to keep the machine moving. All of this is characteristic and typical of *organizational* work, and it precisely corresponds to the requirement of a certain level of knowledge, a certain level of culture, and to a certain capacity for intense attention—that is to say, to the qualities of an organizer. But there is also the direct physical effort: the hands must work in concert with the brain.

At the same time, specialization also ceases to sharply divide workers—this division is transferred to the machines. Working on different machines is, within the basic tenants of "organization," very similar. Thanks to this, communication and mutual understanding are supported through teamwork— through a recognition of common labor. And the possibility of asking each other for help, or giving advice to those in need, is maintained. Here the *comradely* form of cooperation takes shape, upon which the proletariat then builds all its organizations.

This form of collaboration is characterized by the fact that the work of the organizer fuses together with the work of the performer. But it is not specific individuals who are the organizers or performers here —instead it is the *collective*. The tasks are studied, discussed, decided upon, and carried out together; each takes part in the elaboration and realization of their collective will. There, good organization is not achieved by power, nor by submission, but by comradely initiative, collective direction, and comradely discipline on the part of everyone.

The seeds of comradely cooperation have existed in the past, but in our era, it is the first time that it is becoming such a massive force and asserting itself as the fundamental type of organization for an entire class. It deepens as higher technology develops; it expands as the proletarian masses gather in cities—as they become concentrated in gigantic enterprises.

This gathering of the proletariat in the cities and factories has an enormous and complex influence on its psyche. It helps to develop the awareness that, in work —in the struggle with the elements and with life—a person is only one link in a great chain; and that, taken separately, they would be a completely powerless toy to external forces. They would be like a nonviable piece of flesh cut off from a powerful organism. After this realization, the individual "me" self is reduced to its true size and returned to its rightful place.

But this same gathering in cities and factories is accompanied by a very painful tearing away from nature. Nature is, for the proletariat, a force of production and not the source of various living impressions. Moreover, unlike the ruling classes, city life gives the working class very few joys and pleasures. And the aspiration of the proletariat to encounter living nature is all the stronger for it; it can even turn into an intense longing. This is also one of the reasons for their dissatisfaction—for their struggle for new forms of life.

However, comradely cooperation is not a ready-made form. It is scattered everywhere and can be encountered at different stages of development. The comradely consciousness follows in the wake of other stages of development, although it does necessarily lag behind. This is the fundamental axis upon the path of the proletariat, but it is still far from being completed, even in the most advanced countries. Its completion will be achieved under *socialism*, which is nothing other than the comradely organization of the whole life of society.

## VIII.

The spirit of authority, the spirit of individualism, and the spirit of comradeship are three successive types of culture. Proletarian poetry belongs to the third—the highest phase.

The spirit of authority is alien to proletarian poetry, and it cannot help but be hostile towards it. The proletariat is a subordinate class, but it fights against this subordination. Here are verses taken from a workers' newspaper and they are dedicated to one of the political leaders of the proletariat:

> The whole bourgeois order is shaken to its very
> foundations,
> And the world, astonished by such a beautifully
> courageous risk,
> Excitedly watches the genius game,
> To applaud the near victory.
> The world is waiting for the end so it can celebrate
> The fall of rotten, obsolete buildings of the past,
> To start a new era of free days

And to crown every victorious genius in the future.

Whether the author is a worker or not, it is clear that the feelings and thoughts in this poem are not proletarian. A collective that works and struggles together cannot help but value its leaders—its organizers—but only as interpreters for *common* tasks, facilitators of the *common* will of the collective, and as representatives for its *common* strength. But to represent the great world drama of our times as a risky game of chance, in which a genius masterfully plays against other political players, and "the world"—that is, the masses—only "excitedly watch" to then applaud and crown the winner, is to show a purely authoritarian, perhaps even autocratic, understanding of life.

The spirit of individualism, which places the individual "me" at the center of everything, is equally as foreign to the proletariat.

I was always proud,
I was always rebellious,
Sadly, I smiled, but it drove away the gloom
It was always spring, joyously vast,
The specter of night did not frighten my soul
I was always calm, certain, and courageous,
I was intoxicated by the sun, sang songs to the sun,
For such a holy cause, I was not afraid of torture,
And I was consumed in the dazzling idea, as bright as fire

•

And I'm always righteous, clear, and proud.
I walked towards the truth with a cheerful soul,
Ignoring the "difficult," the "painful," and the
"dangerous"!
I lived free, drunk with the struggle
...etc.

It is no coincidence that the initial verse and several other lines in this work—also taken from a workers' newspaper—is almost entirely borrowed from a notoriously bourgeois poet. The very foundation of this poem lacks any creative and collective "we." There is only the old, self-centered, and self-admiring "me." Of course, this is not proletarian poetry.

The proletariat is a very young class, and their art is still in an infantile stage. Even in politics, where their experience is greater, millions of proletarians in Germany, England, and America follow the lead of the bourgeoisie. And it is even easier for proletarian poets to trail behind them. But just as we have the duty to openly declare: "This is not a proletarian policy," the voice of comradely critique must also firmly warn: "This is not proletarian art."

Until now, the poetry of the workers is often not the poetry of the working class. It is not the author who is in question, but their point of view. The poet may, moreover, not belong economically to the working class; but if they have familiarized themselves deeply with collective life, if they have truly and sincerely been imbued with their aspirations, their ideals, their way of thinking, if they rejoice in the joys of the working class and suffer from their suffering—in a word, if they melt into it with all their soul—then they are capable of becoming an artistic spokesperson of the proletariat, an organizer of its forces and of its consciousness in poetic form. Obviously, it is not often that this can happen; and in poetry, even more so than in politics, the proletariat must not rely on allies from outside of their class.

## IX.

Here is a short prose poem by a worker-poet and economist:

### THE WHISTLES

When the morning whistles blow in the working-class suburbs, it is no longer the call of slaves. No, this is the song of the future.
We once labored in miserable workshops, starting work at different times in the morning.
And now, at eight o'clock in the morning, the whistles are screaming for millions.
Millions grab hammers at the same instant.
And their first blows thunder together.

What do the whistles sing?
The anthem of our unity.

A.K. Gastev[10]
*Poetry of the Worker's Blow*

This is lyrical poetry, but not that of the individual "me." For the worker as an isolated individual, the whistles are, of course, a call to forced labor—sometimes they are even an instrument of torture. But for a growing community, this is no longer the case. The "Subject" of this poetry—its real creator, expressing itself through the poet—is not the same as before, and is not found in life. It is the spirit of comradeship.

## THE FUTURE

I overheard the songs of close, joyful ages
In the echoing whirlwind of fiery, immense cities.
I heard the songs of the golden days of the future
In the thunder of factories, in the screams of steel, in the vicious rage of
                    belts.
I saw how our comrades forged golden steel.
And at that moment of the Coming Dawn, wonderful faces
                    appeared.
I know now that all wisdom is in this
                    hammer.
In that firm, persistent, confident hand.

The harder that the resounding hammer beats, crushes,
forges,
The brighter that joy will shine into the gloomy world.
The faster the pistons and gears move,
The more captivating and brighter our days will become.
These songs have been sung to me by millions of voices,
By millions of blacksmiths in blue coats, strong and brave,
The songs are rebellious, red, clear,
ringing.
They announce to everyone that the long night's sleep is
over.
Mighty songs that call to the sun, life, and struggle.
A proud and angry call—vicious, painful
destiny.

V.T. Kirillov[11]
*The Future*[12] No. 1, 1918

The poet's "me" is also on stage here, but he is clearly aware of its role and its place. It intervenes to draw attention to the real initial creator of this poetry (that is to say, the collective) and to draw attention to its real, fundamental creative force (that is to say, organized labor). And the poet does not stop at the level of the proletariat's purely militant, revolutionary shock consciousness, as is the case with most novice worker-poets. This stage of consciousness does not by itself give rise to proletarian poetry—after all, the spirit of this militaristic comradeship is also present in soldiers. The poet goes further and deeper, he reveals the labor consciousness, the cultural consciousness of his class: "beat, crush, forge...The faster the pistons and gears move, the more captivating and brighter our days will become." In combat, there is indeed victory over enemies; but it is only in the development of labor—in the development of the forces of production—that the social ideal is realized.

## X.

Those who conduct experiments often need the support of practical examples. We theorists found ourselves in a difficult situation during a time when there were still few propagandists engaging with the ideas of proletarian art. We found ourselves in a situation in which we had to talk about things we could not find practical examples for—to think about things in which we were unable to say firmly and confidently, "Here is a genuine piece of proletarian art. You can judge other works by this example, and you can make comparisons to it." This is why it is impossible for me not to quote the work which became my first such personal point of reference.

In the newspaper *Pravda,* or in one of its transformations in 1913, a short poem by Samobytnik[13] was published:

## TO A NEW COMRADE

A whirlwind of spinning wheels,
The dance of maddening belts...
Hey, comrade, don't be shy!
Let the chaos of steel scream,
May a sea of tears disappear,
By its dry fire—
Don't be shy!

You came from a peaceful land,
Clear rivers and bright fields...
Hey, comrade, don't be shy!
Here vastness starts to converge,
At the dawn of the coming days...
The impossible has come true—
Don't be shy!

Our happiness has risen,
Along the tops of silvery peaks...
In the realm of sorrow and shadows,
The powerful sun is set ablaze,
And it burns even stronger—
Don't be shy!

Like a stone colossus, you
Stand by the maddening belts...
Let the thunder of the wheels howl,
A link is woven into the chain,
The army closes tightly in—
Don't be shy!

Any problems here do not lie in the artistic quality of the work, in which there is an indisputable and strong talent; that said, this talent is far from being fully developed, and the form could also use some work. But the purity of the content is striking—it is hardly possible to feel and think in a more proletarian way.

The poem takes place under the old order. A factory has hired a novice, coming directly from the countryside—yesterday they were a peasant farmer. What do they represent for a traditional urban worker? A competitor. And, moreover, an inconvenience: they lower the wages because their needs are simple, and they lack experience standing up for themselves—not to mention they have no experience defending common interests. Their thoughts are heavy, their feelings narrow, their will limited, their outlook wretched...And it is difficult to count on them if today or tomorrow there is a need for comradely and united action. And yet, look at how this comrade-poet treats this unexpected new arrival, who is still a stranger.

With what chivalrous attention, with what gentle solicitude, they encourage the timid novice and introduce them into an unfamiliar, incomprehensible, strange, and even terrible world! With what simplicity and power, in concise words but with vivid images, the poet tells them everything they need to know and feel to become a comrade among comrades: the grandiose picture of our current technology as a "chaos of steel," the bitter truth about the "sea of tears" that technology has cost humanity, and the joyous news about the "powerful sun" of the great ideal, of the proud happiness of the common struggle. The memory of a wonderful, distant nature—the "peaceful land, clear rivers, and bright fields" resonates in a touching way. How the heart of the proletariat yearns for nature in the midst of iron and fire, and how rarely this joyful opportunity is available to them! But the willpower of the creative collective is bound to achieve everything in its growing, firm, inevitable efforts...The final chord resonates with victorious certainty:

> A link is woven into the chain,
> The army closes tightly in—
> Don't be shy!

This is the consecration of a new initiate into the fraternity of the Socialist Idea. Is not the poet the organizer of their class?

•

Proletarian poetry is still in its infancy. But it will develop. This development is necessary because the working class needs a complete, holistic self-awareness —and poetry is a part of that awareness.

But even when this poetry grows out of its infancy, the proletariat will not live on it alone. They are the legitimate heir of all the culture of the past, the heir to all that they find best in the poetry of the feudal and bourgeois world.

But the proletariat must seize this heritage in such a way that they do not submit to the spirit of the past which reigns there—as has been the case with every step until now. This inheritance should not reign over the heir but should only be an instrument in their hands. The dead should serve the living, and not hold it back or paralyze it.

This is why the proletariat needs its *own* poetry, so as not to submit to a foreign poetic consciousness, strong in its centuries-old maturity. The proletariat must have its own poetic consciousness, the clarity of which must be immutable. This new consciousness must unfold and embrace the whole world, the whole of life, with its creative unity.

May proletarian poetry grow and mature and teach the working class to be what history intended it to be: a fighter and a destroyer only out of external necessity —but a creator in all of its nature.

## NOTES

1. In feudal Russia, *mir* was the word for a rural peasant commune. The word *mir* also means "the world" and "peace" in Russian. It is likely not an accident, nor a coincidence, that Bogdanov chose this word to illustrate his point.

2. Afanasy Afanasyevich Fet (1820–1892), also known as Shenshin, was the son of nobility and a famous lyrical poet in Russia. His romantic poetry largely centered on love, nature, beauty, and death, but he was often criticized for not putting any political or social content into his poems. This led to accusations that he was creating "art for art's sake." Later in his life, he also worked to translate Arthur Schopenhauer, Heinrich Heine, and Johann Wolfgang von Goethe into Russian. Personally, he was a conservative and a demanding landowner, in sharp contrast to his flowery poems.

3. *Barskaya* is a Russian word meaning "lord" or "lordly."

4. Nikolai Alexeyevich Nekrasov (1821–1878) was a Russian poet and journalist whose work largely centered on compassionately highlighting the suffering of the Russian peasantry through sentimental prose and realistic satire—his most famous works being "Red-Nosed Frost" (*Moroz krasni-nos*) and "Who Can Be Happy and Free in Russia?" (*Komu na Rusi zhit khorosho?*). He owned and edited the famous literary magazine founded by Alexander Pushkin called *The Contemporary* (*Sovremennik*), which was suppressed by the Tsar after its subeditor Nikolai Chernyshevsky (author of the famous 1863 novel *What Is to Be Done?*) began to develop the magazine into an organ of militant radicalism. Nekrasov then took over the journal *Notes of the Fatherland* (*Otechestvenniye zapiski*), where he remained until his death.

5. Alexey Mikhailovich Gmyrev (1887–1911) was a worker-poet— the son of a railway worker—whose mother died when he was 9

and whose father met the same fate when Gmyrev was 15. He worked in a factory to support himself, and in 1903, at the age of 16, he became engaged in revolutionary politics and joined the Russian Social Democratic Labor Party. He was arrested that same year but escaped from prison. He began writing poetry in 1905 after the first Russian Revolution. In May of 1906, he was exiled to Arkhangelsk Oblast in northeastern Russia, and in 1908, he was accused of murder and sentenced to hard labor in Kherson Oblast in present-day southern Ukraine. He died there in 1911 of tuberculosis. He was 24 years old. Although less than 10 of his poems were published during his lifetime, his works began to be printed in the revolutionary newspapers *Zvezda* and *Pravda* starting in 1912.

6. People's Will (*Narodnaya volya*) was a secret revolutionary group consisting largely of young socialist intellectuals who decided to split with the group Land and Freedom (*Zemlya i volya*) in 1879 over a disagreement about revolutionary tactics (see endnote 7). People's Will believed that terrorism—mainly through targeting hated government officials for assassination—had the power to both overthrow the autocratic regime and initiate a peasant uprising. The group was heavily influenced by the Russian nihilist, revolutionary terror theorist, and communist Sergey Gannadiyevich Nechayev (1847–1882) and Italian socialist and "propaganda of the deed" theorist Carlo Pisacane (1818–1857). The group succeeded in assassinating Tsar Alexander II in March of 1881, which led to a wave of repression and executions. Despite this, People's Will continued to operate clandestinely. In fact, Vladimir Lenin's older brother—Alexander Ulyanov—was a prominent member of People's Will and was executed for his role in attempting to assassinate Tsar Alexander III in 1887.

7. Land and Freedom (*Zemlya i volya*) was a secret revolutionary group between the years of 1861–1864 before emerging from the

underground and reconstituting itself as a political party in 1876. In 1879, it disintegrated due to political splits. The group was a proponent of a peasant-oriented socialist populism (*narodnichestvo*), believing that the rural peasantry was the principal revolutionary force in Russia. The group's leadership, however, consisted mostly of young, urban intelligentsia. Their political program culminated in their "call to the people" (*khozhdeniye v narod*) campaign in which revolutionaries were made to settle into rural parts of the Russian Empire and begin distributing revolutionary literature while organizing the workers and peasants. Debates over the use of terrorism and assassination led the group to split into several factions, with People's Will (*Narodnaya volya*) representing the most violent offshoot (see endnote 6).

8. *Bylina*—plural *byliny*—were Russian forms of heroic oral poetry that flourished in the 10th–12th centuries. The word *bylina* comes from the word for the past tense of "to be" (*byl*) implying these were epic songs based on "something that was."

9. "The Tale of Igor's Campaign" (*Slovo o polku Igoreve*) is an epic poem written in Old East Slavic sometime in the late 12th century. It recounts the unsuccessful armed struggles between Igor Svyatoslavich, a Rus' Prince, and Turkic nomads known as the Polovtsians (also known as the Kipchak, or Cumans) in the Don River region in Russia.

10. Aleksei Kapitonovich Gastev (1882–1939) was a revolutionary, proletarian poet, and pioneer of scientific management. He began his revolutionary activity at a young age while he was attending the Moscow Pedagogical Institute. After he was expelled for participating in revolutionary activities, he joined the Russian Social Democratic Labor Party in 1901 and became an early supporter of the Bolshevik faction, corresponding often with Vladimir Lenin and his wife Nadezhda Krupskaya on Party policy—as well as reporting directly to them about his agitation efforts. He actively

participated in the Russian Revolution of 1905, leading a fighting unit in Kostroma and inciting strikes in the cities of Yaroslavl, Ivanovo, and Rostov. He was arrested and exiled three times but was able to escape and live illegally in Russia each time. In 1913, he joined the Circle of Proletarian Culture with his friend Anatoly Lunacharsky, and by 1917, he became active within the Proletarian Culture (Proletkult) movement that Bogdanov helped found. In 1918, a collection of his prose poetry *Poetry of the Worker's Blow* (*Poeziia rabochego udara*) was the first book published by Proletkult. In 1920, he abandoned writing poetry altogether, instead founding and directing the Central Institute of Labor (*Tsentral'nyy institut truda*), calling it his "last work of art." With Lenin's encouragement and an allocation of state funding, the institute began to develop (some might say Taylorist) methods of training workers to perform mechanical operations in the most efficient ways possible. This was done by recording their movements with photography and movie cameras multiple times and analyzing them for a common mechanical rhythm (for more on this, see Velminski 2017). On September 8, 1938, Gastev was arrested and charged with "counter-revolutionary terrorist activity." On April 14, 1939, he was tried and convicted. The next day, he was shot to death in the suburbs of Moscow.

11. Vladimir Timofeyevitch Kirillov was a proletarian poet born into the peasantry in 1889 or 1890. He became politically active as a boy and participated in the Russian Revolution of 1905 after joining the Russian Social Democratic Labor Party. He was subsequently arrested in 1906 and exiled to Siberia. He first published poems in 1913 and soon after became associated with Proletarian Culture (Proletkult). He was elected to Proletkult's national presidium in 1918. In 1920, he left Proletkult with a group of other artists to form the literary circle The Forge (*Kuznitsa*). In 1921, he vocally opposed the New Economic Policy and left the

Communist Party. In 1937, he was arrested and jailed. Kirillov was executed sometime between 1937–1943 in either Moscow or Smolensk.

12. *The Future* (*Gryadushcheye*) was the organ of the Petrograd Proletkult from 1918–1920.

13. Aleksei Ivanovich Mashirov (1884–1943), better known by his alias Samobytnik, was a proletarian poet and journalist. Like the other worker-poets mentioned thus far, he participated in the Russian Revolution of 1905. In 1908, he joined the Russian Social Democratic Labor Party, and in 1912, he was employed as a journalist at the newspaper *Pravda*, which caught the attention of the Tsarist government. After multiple arrests, he was exiled to Siberia in 1916, where he remained until his liberation following the February Revolution in 1917. In 1919, he helped found the Petrograd Proletkult with Bogdanov and others. He also became an active writer with the literary circle "The Forge" (*Kuznitsa*) and the Proletkult journal "The Future" (*Gryadushcheye*). Throughout the 1920s and 1930s, he held high positions in the field of culture: for most of the 1920s, he was the Chairman of the Leningrad Council of Art Workers; from 1930–1933, he was the Director of the Leningrad Conservatory; and from 1937 until his death, he was the head of the Leningrad Institute of Theater and Music. He died during the Nazi Siege of Leningrad in 1943.

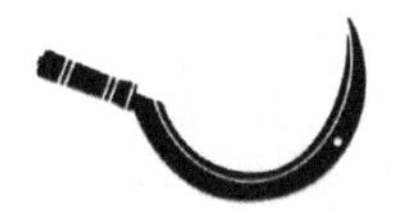

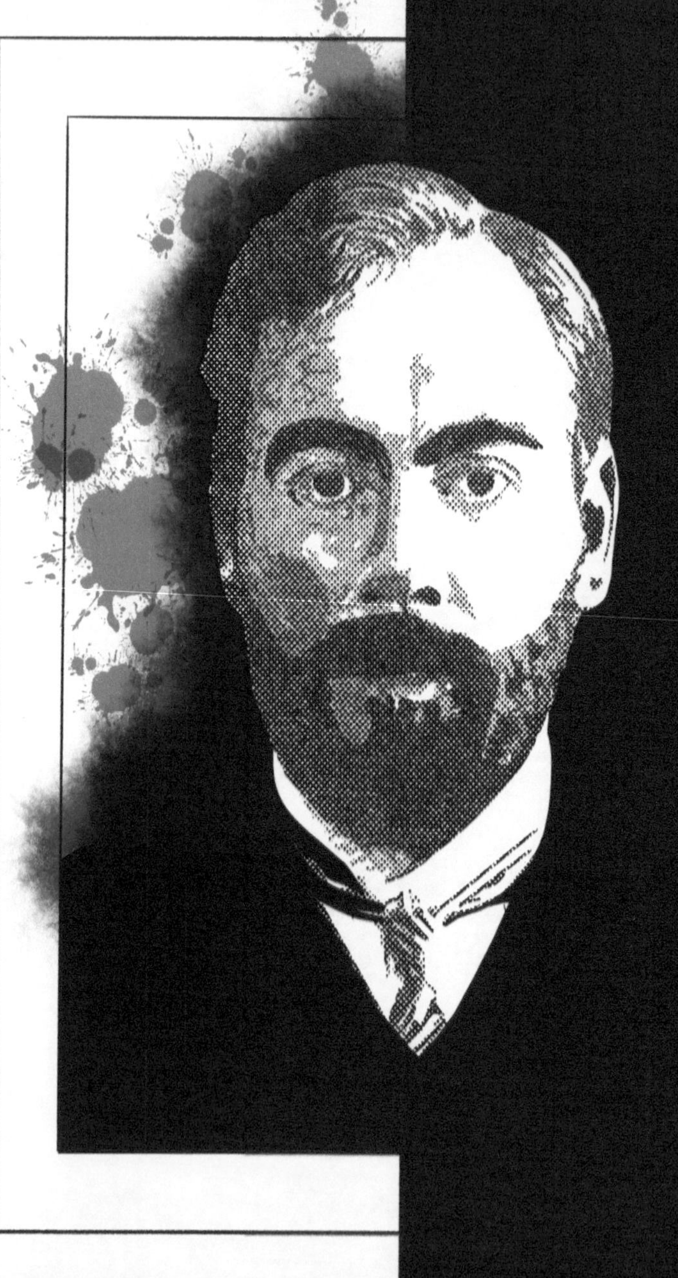

# 2

# On Artistic Heritage

There are two daunting artistic tasks facing the working class. The first is independent creativity: to recognize oneself and to recognize the world in harmonious and living images—in other words, to organize one's spiritual forces in an artistic form. The second task is how to navigate one's heritage: to seize the wealth of art, to possess that which was created in the past, and make that which is admirable into one's own without submitting to the spirit of feudal or bourgeois society that is reflected within it. This second task is no less difficult than the first. Let us explore some general ways to solve it.

## I.

A believer who studies a foreign religion seriously and attentively exposes themselves to the danger of going astray or adopting something heretical from the point of view of their own faith. It has happened on several occasions to Christian scholars who studied Buddhism and have themselves become quite Buddhist —or at least they have incorporated certain Buddhist moral teachings into their lives. The reverse has also happened. But let us suppose that the same religious systems are studied by a free thinker[1] who sees a similarity of poetic creation in all religions—that one religion does not contain the whole truth, but only part of it. Are they threatened with the same danger as, say, a religious scientist? Of course not. They can grasp, with the greatest of enthusiasm, the beauties and depths of its teachings. And while these religions have subjugated hundreds of millions of people, the free thinker understands them *not from a religious point of view*. Instead, they are able to appreciate these teachings from a different, higher point of view. The enormous wealth of knowledge and emotion structured within Buddhism might affect their heart and mind more than the heart and mind of a learned Christian, who, through study, is unable to shake off the latent resistance of their own faith in their struggle against what would be perceived as "temptation." But for the free thinker, this temptation to become a believing Buddhist does not exist because these foreign religious ideas do not engage with the same part of their consciousness that processes religious material.

Both Christians and free thinkers understand

Buddhism "critically." But the fundamental difference lies in the *type*, the basis, the "criteria" of their criticism. The believer is not above their own subject of study, but instead they are more or less on the same level. They criticize from the point of view of their own dogma and feelings. They look for contradictions in other people's myths, in other cults, in other moral revelations; and, upon finding these contradictions, they are unable to appreciate the often hidden poetic truths they harbor. Therefore, if they are able to penetrate into this poetry, they will pay the price of facing an internal contradiction—a contradiction within themselves— they will "fall into temptation." For the believer, Buddhism cannot be a shared cultural heritage from a foreign world; and if the Christian believer understands the Buddhist faith with sympathy, it therefore has the potential to subdue them and force them to abandon Christianity.

The situation is not much better for the fierce atheist—a representative of the progressive, but still underdeveloped, bourgeois consciousness—who sees in every religion only superstition and deception. This "believer but in reverse" lurks above religion just enough to reject it, but not enough to understand it. For the atheist too, religion cannot be within their heritage; and, worst-case scenario, it becomes a temptation only if they sense within it something which *is not only* deception and superstition—however, they would be unable to understand exactly what that kernel of truth might be.

In another situation, our free thinker is the representative of the highest level that bourgeois consciousness is capable of reaching. Their understanding of religious work, as a work of popular poetry, enables them—within the limits of this point of view—to evaluate their subject freely and impartially. For them, there are no difficult internal contradictions in seeing, for example, that the depth of ideas in Manu's law among the ancient Aryans of India are, in many ways, superior to the dogmas of ancient and modern Christianity; or that the Hindu attitude toward death, expressed through funeral rites, surpasses without comparison the Christian attitude toward death in both its greatness and beauty. Free from religious consciousness in general—and waging a struggle against it whenever it obscures thought and alters the will of the people—the free thinker, at the same time, is capable of making all religions a valuable cultural heritage for themselves and for others.

The attitude of the proletarian toward the culture of the past—the culture of the bourgeois world and the feudal world—passes through similar stages. In the beginning, it is simply culture—culture in the broadest sense of the term. The proletarian does not imagine anything else; they stand immersed within this culture. In their science and philosophy there may be errors; within art there may be inaccurate motives; and in morality and law there may be injustices—but for them, none of this is linked to the essence of culture. Instead, they are mistakes, deviations, and imperfections that would be corrected through progressive development. And then, if the proletarian notices within their culture a "bourgeois aspect" or "aristocracy," then they understand them only in the sense that those elements are *protecting the interests* of the ruling classes, a defense that falsifies culture—but the very method and point of view of this culture, that is to say, its essence, are left without a shadow of a doubt. They are unable to obtain an objective view and instead try to assimilate "what is good in it." They are no more protected from the temptations of Christianity than is the Buddhist or the Brahmin who studies Christianity, or vice versa. They are infused with the old ways of thinking and feeling— all the attitudes and viewpoints of the world are instilled within them. Their own proletarian-class point of view is retained only where, and insofar as, the voice of *class interest* is able to speak clearly and sufficiently and powerfully. When this clarity and conviction does not exist—when the question posed by life is difficult and complex, especially if it is a recent problem—then it is not resolved independently: either a ready-made decision is simply taken from someone within their surrounding social environment or someone sheds light on the proletarian class interest from their own point of view. Both positions were clearly manifested in the attitudes of the working intelligentsia in European countries when [World War I] broke out: some surrendered, almost without reason, to the wave of patriotism; others were able to "recognize" that the greater interests of the working class required unity with the bourgeoisie in the name of defending and saving both the fatherland and domestic production because "the collapse of both would reverse the progress made by both the working class and the whole of their civilization."

This grandiose and cruel experience fully illuminates that when the proletarian attitude toward the world—their way of thinking, their all-encompassing point of view—is not developed, then it is not the proletarian collective which takes possession of the culture of the past as their heritage, but rather they take possession of it as merely contrasting cultural fodder to use uncritically for their own immediate objectives.

If the proletarian convinces themselves of this, and arrives at some kind of absolute, anarchist denial of the old culture—that is, they refuse their heritage—then they take the position of a naïve atheist in relation to religious heritage. But it gets even worse, because it is possible for the bourgeois atheist to be satisfied without understanding religion; indeed, they have other cultural supports to fall back on, and the only thing that suffers is their breadth of thought and scope of creativity. Meanwhile, the worker has nothing of equivalence to oppose the rich cultivated culture of the enemy camp, for they are unable to create something entirely new that is of the same magnitude. So, when older cultural touchstones remain solely in the hands of their enemies, it is a superior instrument—a weapon directed against the working class.

The conclusion is clear. It is necessary for the working class to find, develop, and carry out a viewpoint that is superior to the culture of the past, just as the viewpoint of the free thinker is superior to the world of religion. It will then become possible to take hold of this culture without submitting to it, to make it a tool for the construction of a new life, and a weapon in the struggle against the society of old.

## II.

It was Karl Marx who laid down the foundational understanding that the old world is possessed by spiritual forces. The revolution he carried out in the fields of social science and philosophy consisted of questioning the fundamental methods of these disciplines, and he found new results that were obtained from a higher point of view, which was also a proletarian class point of view. It was from bourgeois sources that Marx drew at least nine-tenths of not only the source material for his titanic edifice, but also the methods of their elaboration: from classical bourgeois economics, inspection reports of English factories, the petite-bourgeois criticism of capital by Sismondi[2] and Proudhon[3]; in fact, he drew from almost all of the utopian socialist thinkers—he engaged with the dialectic of German idealism, the materialism of the French Enlightenment and of Feuerbach, the social constructions of class by French historians, and the brilliant descriptions of class psychology by Balzac, etc., etc. All of this took a different form than the bourgeois source material and was arranged according to new relations; it was turned into an instrument for the construction of a proletarian organization, into a weapon in the struggle against the rule of capital.

How could such a miracle happen?

First, Marx established that society itself is the organization of production, and upon this rests the basis of all societal laws and all forms of its development. This is the point of view of the socially producing class, *the point of view of collective labor*. From this point of view, Marx subjected the knowledge of the past to critique, and having purified its material—having melted it in the fires of his ideas—he created from it a proletarian knowledge: scientific socialism.

Here, then, is the way in which the cultural creation of the past can be transformed into the effective heritage of the working class: by *critically reworking it from the point of view of collective labor*. And this is how Marx himself understood the question; it is not a coincidence that he called his main work *Capital: A Critique of Political Economy*.

And this is by no means limited to the social sciences. In all areas of study, our method for both obtaining and assimilating cultural heritage is *proletarian class critique*.

## III.

Let us fully elucidate the bases of our critique, that is to say, the essence of collective labor's point of view.

A social process can be broken down into three

points—or, perhaps, more precisely, it has three sides or aspects—technical, economic, and ideological. For the technical aspect, society struggles with nature and subdues it—that is to say, we *organize the outside world* in the interests of our life and development. For the economic aspect, *it is organized by itself* through the relations of collaboration and distribution between people in their struggle with nature. For the ideological aspect, we *organize our own emotions and experiences* and from there we create organizational tools to use throughout all our development and lives. Therefore, every task within the sphere of technology, economy, and ideology is an *organizational* task—and moreover, it is a *social* task.

There are no exceptions to this. For example, the army sets for itself the goal of destruction, extermination, and disorganization; but this is a *means*, not the ultimate goal. The ultimate goal is to reorganize the world according to the interests of the community to which the army belongs. Or, to put it another way, the artist-individual may imagine that they create their work for themselves; but if they really created it for themselves alone—and if they did not organize collective feelings—their work would not be interesting or necessary for anyone except the artist-individual themselves. It would have no relation to spiritual culture—it would be just like a dream, in that even if an individual's dream is beautiful, it is unable to be transmitted to another person. If the artist-individual only created for themselves—if they attempted to create art without using the materials, the processing methods, the embodiment, and the expressions received from their social environment— then they would, in fact, create absolutely nothing at all.

So, the point of view of collective labor is *pan-organizational*. It cannot be otherwise from the point of view of the working class, which organizes external matter into a product, and through its work, it organizes itself into a creative and militant collective. This cooperation and class struggle leads the working class to organize its experience into class consciousness—in all their way of life and in all of their creation—and to them alone history entrusts a mission: to organize the entire life of humanity both integrally and harmoniously.

# IV.

Let us go back to our first example. Should the entire world of religious creativity become the cultural heritage for the working class, even though, until now, the whole of religion has obviously served as an instrument of their enslavement? What is the use of such heritage? And what should the working class do with it?

Our critique thus far provides a clear and comprehensive answer to this question.

Religion is the solution to an ideological problem for a specific type of collective—namely, an authoritarian one. This is a collective built upon authoritarian cooperation, on the separation of the roles of those who "direct" and those who "execute"; it is built upon power—that is, upon submission. Likewise, a similar organizational model was used for patriarchal clan communities in feudal society; these models were also used for the institutions of serfdom and slavery, the bureaucratic-police state, the modern army, and, to a lesser extent, the bourgeois family. Finally, capital also builds its corporations upon these models of power, and therefore, upon models of submission.

What is the organizational task of ideology? It is to organize the experience of the collective, in a harmonious and holistic manner, and in accordance with its structure, so that the resulting cultural products themselves, in turn, serve as organizational tools to preserve, formalize, consolidate, and further develop a given type of community organization. If we understand this, then it is easy to understand how an authoritarian way of structuring life works all this out.

This authoritarian system is simply transposed into the realm of experience and thought. Every action, every phenomenon—whether natural or human—is presented as the combination of two links: an active organizing desire and a passive realization. The whole world thinks of itself in the image of an authoritarian society: above it, there is the supreme authority, the "deity," and sprouting from the supreme authority is a complicated, successive chain of subordinate authorities, one after the other—lower gods, "demigods," "saints," etc.—who rule different sectors and areas of life. And all these representations are saturated with authoritarian feelings and states of mind: admiration, obedience, respectful fear. This is the religious relationship to the world: quite simply, it is an authoritarian ideology.

It is quite understandable why religion is the perfect organizational tool for an authoritarian way of life. It directly introduces a person into this system, it deposits them in a specific place within it, and it disciplines them to fulfill the role that the system has predetermined for them in advance. One's personality merges organically with the social whole in a unity of feeling, thought, and practice. This unity then acquires an indestructible coherence.

The form of religious creation is predominantly poetic. Our free thinker correctly noted this, without however grasping the main point: the social content of religion. At the stage of development when religions are taking shape, poetry is not yet freed from the matrix of theoretical and practical knowledge. Religion then encompasses everything—all of knowledge—and organizes the entire experience of humankind. Knowledge in general is then understood as a revelation from society—either directly, or through intermediaries.

One may ask: what sort of heritage is religious culture for the working class? It is an important and very valuable one. It becomes an instrument for the working class after it has passed through their critical gaze—but not an instrument to be maintained. Instead, it can be used by the working class in order to *understand* all that is authoritarian in life. The authoritarian world has had its day, but it is not dead. Its vestiges surround us on all sides, sometimes openly— but more often than not, it stealthily uses all sorts of protective, and sometimes most unexpected, disguises. To defeat such an enemy, one must know it—and know it deeply and seriously.

It is not just a question about refuting religious doctrines—although with this new critique, the worker will find themselves incomparably better armed than the enraged but naïve atheist, who refutes the faith of others with logical calculations or childish assertions that religion was invented by priests to rob people. What is even more important is that the possession of this heritage gives the working class the possibility of correctly estimating the significance of the authoritarian elements in today's society, its mutual connections, and its relation to social development.

If religion is a tool for preserving authoritarian organization, the role that it plays in class relations is clear. The piety of the workers is, for example, a means of reinforcing their submission, of maintaining in them respect for discipline, which the ruling classes need in order to ensure their exploitation—no matter what various religious socialists may say about the matter. It is clear that the formula adopted by many workers' parties—that "religion is a private matter"—is nothing more than a temporary political compromise. The constant union between the saber and the cassock—the military and the church—becomes understandable: both are strictly authoritarian organizations. The attachment of the petite-bourgeois and patriarchal peasant families to religion—to the "law of God"—is also explained; and at the same time, the enormous danger of these kinds of persisting authoritarian cells turns out to be an enormous danger for social progress.

It is in this new light that the problem of the role of party leaders—that is to say, the authorities—and the significance of collective control over them is revealed, etc., etc.

On the other hand, there is also the artistic richness of people's experiences, crystallized in all sorts of sacred traditions and scriptures—paintings of a strange and peculiar life, harmonious in their own way, that expand the horizons of a person, deeply introducing humanity to the movements of the world, promoting a new, independent creation, free from their familiar environment and habits of thought...

Is it worth it for the working class to absorb their religious heritage?

## V.

I deliberately started with a rather controversial and difficult topic. But this makes it easier to sort out our main problem: the question of the artistic heritage of the past. It is clear that critique is the instrument which must be mastered by the working class, with its new, pan-organizational, collective point of view of labor.

So how does it approach this subject?

The soul of artistic work is what we call its "artistic

idea." By this I mean the artist's idea and the essence of its implementation—in other words, it is a problem, as well as a principle of its own solution. What is the nature of this problem? Now we know: no matter how the artist looks at it, it is always an *organizational* problem. Moreover, this problem always takes two forms: 1) it is a matter of harmoniously and holistically organizing the elements of one's life and experience; and 2) that the whole, which is created through this organization of life and experience, should itself serve as an organizational instrument for a certain collective. Without the first part, we would not be dealing with art, only gibberish; without the second, the work would be neither interesting nor necessary for anyone except the artist themselves.

As an illustration, we will take one of the greatest works of world literature, a most beautiful gem from the cultural heritage of old: Shakespeare's *Hamlet*.

What does this artistic idea consist of? It consists of formulating and finding a solution for the organizational problem of the human soul, which is bifurcated in life by a difficult contradiction: 1) the desire for happiness, love, and a harmonious life; and 2) the need to wage a painful, harsh, ruthless struggle. But how do we get out of this contradiction? How do we reconcile with it? How can we ensure that a thirst for harmony does not weaken a person to the inevitable struggles of life—that it does not deprive them of the necessary strength, firmness, and composure that is needed? And at the same time, how do we ensure that the harshness of what life inflicts upon us—the blows, the blood, the dirt in our wounds—does not destroy all the joy, all the beauty of existence? How do we restore the unity and integrity of the soul, which has been torn in twain by the sharp collision between one's deepest and highest needs and the imperious demand dictated by the hostilities of the surrounding environment?

We see at the outset how grand the scale of this organizational task, how enormous and universal its significance for humanity. Of course, we are not referring only to the Danish Prince Hamlet, nor to the countless "Ham-lites" of our petite-bourgeois literature. This task is an inevitable moment in the development of every person; those who have the strength to resolve it are raised to a higher level of self-awareness; for those whose strength is lacking, it becomes a source of spiritual destruction and sometimes even death. Perhaps more acutely than anything, this tragedy penetrates the soul of the idealist proletarian, and even into the collective psyche of the working class. Fraternity is its ideal—the harmony of life for all humanity is its highest goal. But since the surrounding environment is far from this ideal, a difficult, sometimes dark, and cruel struggle is imposed on the working class, all while they are under the constant threat of losing everything that they have achieved through previous struggles—all while under the threat of losing their social dignity and their very meaning of life. Few are the joys they are given, but great is their thirst for them—and the inevitable spontaneity of social hostility and anarchy threatens to take away or poison what little joys they do possess. Throughout the fierceness of this struggle—in the despair of defeat, in the rage of retaliatory strikes—is not the very capacity to love and to be happy fundamentally undermined at its root?

It is on this basis that the tragedy of Hamlet unfolds. He is a richly gifted man, with a fine artistic nature, and at the same time spoiled by life. He enjoyed the upbringing of a prince—and the heir to the throne—and for several years wandered Germany as a student. On the one hand, he was in a cheerful, comradely environment, able to enjoy everything that science and art had to offer. And on the other hand, he had a light and poetic love with Ophelia. Rarely has someone on earth achieved such an existence so full of happiness and harmony. Hamlet was accustomed to this; he had not tried to live in any other way, and he could not imagine anything else. But as time passed, the horror and vileness of life crept up on him; first as a dull premonition, then as painful evidence.

His family was destroyed, and the legal order of his country was shaken to its foundations. The fratricide-traitor seized his father's throne and seduced his mother; hypocrisy, intrigue, and debauchery reigned at court; the decline of good, older morality spread throughout the country, giving rise to unrest. It became necessary to restore the law, put an end to crimes, avenge the death of his father and the shame inflicted upon his family. For Hamlet, this is all an immutable duty determined by the entire structure of his feudal consciousness.

Does he have the necessary strength to do this? Yes, his rich nature possesses it because he is not only an artist and a favorite of fate—he is not only a "passive aesthete." He is also the son of a warrior-king and a descendant of the formidable Vikings; therefore, he has already received an excellent education in soldiery. There is a fighter in him, but it has not yet been revealed; he has not been put to the test, and even worse, this fighter is within the same body as the passive aesthete.

And this is the essence of the tragedy. The struggle demands Hamlet to be cunning, deceitful, violent, and cruel, which is repugnant to his soft and tender soul. Additionally, these demands must be directed against the people closest and most dear to him: his beloved mother turns out to be in the enemy camp, and Ophelia becomes a weapon of intrigue against him. His enemies push his loved ones forward, like experienced strategists, skillfully taking advantage of the weak points in his soul. His hand raised for the blow freezes, an internal struggle paralyzes his will, momentary resolve is replaced by hesitation and inaction—time is running out while he engages in fruitless disputes with himself. There takes root a deep split in his personality which leads to a temporary collapse: everything gets mixed up in the chaos of hopeless contradictions and Hamlet "goes crazy."

An ordinary person would have died right there without doing much of anything. But Hamlet is an extraordinary, heroic figure. Through the torments of despair, despite a serious illness of the soul, he nevertheless, step by step, advances towards a real decision. The two elements of his personality—the warrior and the aesthete—pierce each other and begin to merge into a new unity: an active aesthete, a fighter for the harmony of life. The fundamental contradiction disappears. The thirst for harmony takes the form of militant effort, the blood and dust of the struggle is redeemed immediately by a conscious purification of life, and it rises to a higher level. The organizational task has been solved; the artistic idea has taken shape.

It is true, however, that Hamlet dies; and in this, the great poet is, as always, objective and sincere. Hamlet's enemies had one advantage: while he gathered the strength of his soul, they acted and prepared for his downfall. But he dies victorious; crime has been punished, legal order restored, and the fate of Denmark passes into safe hands—those of the young hero Fortinbras, a man less important than Hamlet, but just as completely and entirely imbued with the principles of this feudal world; the same ideas that animated Hamlet.

Here we come to the next point in our critique. The organizational task has been posed and solved; but which collective gave the author the vital material for his work? It was not, of course, the proletariat, which did not exist at the time. The author of *Hamlet*, whoever he really was (as we know, this is a controversial issue) was either an aristocrat himself or was an ardent supporter of the aristocracy: it is from this world that he draws most of the content for his plays. They are all marked with the monarchical-feudal ideal: power and obedience, faith in the will of a deity who governs the world, belief in the holiness and in the immutability of the established order that has existed since time immemorial, the recognition of some people as superior beings, destined by their very birth to lead and govern, while other lower beings are destined to be led, incapable of any role other than submission. Would not these facts destroy the value of this work for the working class?

I will answer with a question: is it necessary for the working class to know other organizational types besides their own? Is it possible to develop and formalize their own organizational type in any other way than by comparing and contrasting them with differing organizational types—other than criticizing and reworking them, or repurposing certain elements? And who better than a great master artist to introduce and lead the working class into the very depths of this alien organization of life and thought? The role of our critique is to show its historical significance, its link with the lowest level of development, and its contradictions with the living conditions and tasks of the proletariat. Once this is done, there is no longer any danger of succumbing to the influence of this foreign type of organization; knowledge of this type becomes one of the most valuable tools for building a working class type of organization.

And here the objectivity of the great artist gives the best support for critique. All the conservatism of the authoritarian world, including its fundamental mediocrity, and the weakness it imparts upon human consciousness, is revealed through nothing other than itself. It is worth recalling in *Hamlet* the first appearance of the hero Fortinbras—he is the impetus for Hamlet to examine his soul and pave the way towards the solution to his problem. Proudly, convinced that he is right, and without any doubt or hesitation, Fortinbras leads his army to conquer some piece of land that is not worth, perhaps, the blood of the last soldier to die in his war...

Finally, of tremendous importance is the fact that the organizational task in this work is posed and solved based on life in a foreign society. Nevertheless, the solution, in its general form, remains valid for life today, and for the proletariat as a class—wherever the thirst for harmony comes up against the dryness of the demands of the struggle. There, art teaches the working class to identify an overall direction and a universal solution for organizational problems: this is indispensable for the working class to be able to realize its world organizational ideal.

## VI.

The Belgian artist Constantin Meunier[4] represented in his sculptures the life of workers and their daily labors. His statue "The Philosopher" depicts a worker-philosopher deep in thought with some important philosophical question. The nude figure produces a solid and strong impression of someone who is focused intensely upon a single problem, overcoming some great unseen resistance.

What is the artistic idea of this statue? Its organizational task is this: how does one combine and link together hard physical labor with the work of thought, with the creation of ideas? Here is a way to solve it... Let us take a look at the figure of the "philosopher," who exemplifies a kind of restrained effort, in which every visible muscle is full of tension—but this straining is not from external effort, it is from turning inward to the depths of oneself and subsequently having the solution spring forth, full of conviction: "*thought itself is a physical effort*; its nature is similar to the labor of teaching; there are no contradictions between mental and physical labor, their division is artificial and fleeting." Scientific research from physiology and psychology fully confirms this idea; but this conclusion is much closer to the truth, and much more understandable, in its artistic embodiment. And its enormous importance for the proletariat needs no demonstration.

But our critique must raise the following question: from which social group—from which class—does the artist adopt their point of view? As it turns out, although he portrays the point of view of the workers, he is not an ideologue of the working *class* because he does not portray the point of view of *collective labor*. This worker-philosopher is an artist-individual; one does not feel, or only very vaguely— almost imperceptibly— feels the connections that merge the effort of his thoughts with the physical and spiritual effort of millions of workers, each of whom work as a link within the world chain of labor. This artist is an intellectual in terms of his social status; he is used to working alone, without noticing the extent to which his work—its origins, methods, and tasks—stem from the entire collective labor of humankind. In this way, the point of view of the working intelligentsia differs little from that of the bourgeois intelligentsia: it is just as individualistic. And it is here that our critique completes what the artist was unable to give us.

## VII.

When faced with the art of the past, the tasks of proletarian critique therefore define themselves. By pursuing them, it gives the working class the opportunity to firmly master—and independently use —the organizational experience of thousands of centuries of human labor that have crystallized in particular artistic forms.

The typical understanding of the role and meaning of proletarian critique is generally not taken in this way. More often than not, it strays from the position of "civic art" on the question of its significance for agitation and propaganda in the defense of class interests. Several years ago, the worker Ivan Kubikov,[5] urging proletarians to study the best works of old-world literature, analyzed its educational influence as follows: without a doubt, it contains "not only pure gold, but also elements of 'ore' that is harmful to the proletariat," namely, "conservative, moderating forces." However, according to Kubikov, this is not as terrible as it sounds because the workers possess a class instinct which enables them to successfully separate the gold from the ore. Kubikov continues:

> If we look closely at the impressions that we get from art, we will see that the gold rings true, and the remaining ore misses the consciousness of the worker... I have personally been amazed while observing the way an oppositionally minded worker sometimes manages to draw revolutionary conclusions from the most innocent works of art.

> *Our Dawn*,[6] No. 3, 1914, p. 48–49

This is a naïve point of view and is fundamentally flawed.

There is little good that can come from such an instinct which "manages" to draw revolutionary conclusions from a truly innocent work. Misrepresentation is misrepresentation. What does this distortion indicate? That the power of immediate feelings, and a lack of objectivity, naturally subdues thought and critique. Is this really what the consciousness of the class whose task it is to solve the world organizational problem should be?

Kubikov takes [Friedrich] Schiller's *Don Carlos* as his example of the "gold-ore" ratio. He says that the denunciation of tyranny and the fiery speeches made by the Marquis of Posa are the gold; but the fact that the Marquis dreams of an absolute monarchy, albeit enlightened and humane, is the ore. This is wrong. These "fiery words"—by which I mean vague words spoken with weakness of thought—allow the reader to perfectly educate themselves on the direction of this revolutionary phrasing. On the other hand, the artistic and profound living expression of the ideal of enlightened absolutism, for the historically conscious reader, is by no means an "ore" from the point of view of proletarian critique. This ideal is a model of intellectual organization; to know and understand such past models is necessary for the organizing class of the future. In the struggle of the hero-personalities introduced by the artist, it is necessary to understand the struggle of the social forces which determined the consciousness and the will of the people at that time—as well as to understand the need for certain ideals that arise from the nature of these social forces. Utilizing art to penetrate into the soul of those classes which have disappeared—or are currently disappearing—from history, as well as the classes which currently occupy the world stage, is one of the best ways to take possession of the accumulated cultural and organizational experiences of humanity. This is the most precious heritage for the working class.

Insofar as the art of the past is capable of fostering certain feelings and moods of the proletariat, it should serve as a means of deepening and enlightening them; a means of widening their purview to cover the whole life of humanity—but not as a means of agitation, not as a tool for propaganda.

•

The critic who is able to convey to the proletariat a great work of the old culture—for example, in the theatre, after the performance of a brilliant play, if they are able to interpret its meaning and value from an organizational, collective labor point of view—or, if they are able to give a short and accessible interpretation that explains a performance, or highlights an article in a workers' newspaper, or a poem published in a workers' magazine, or a novel by a great master, then this critic will do a serious, necessary, and useful service for the working class.

And here exists an immense field of work—necessary and indispensable work—that, at the same time, will always be reliable since the labor of critique will never disappear.

# NOTES

1. For the sake of fidelity, the phrase "free thinker" *(svobodnyy myslitel')* has been translated literally despite the reactionary undertones it carries in the 21st century. During Bogdanov's time, a "free thinker" would have simply referred to someone skeptical of religious thought, as opposed to a phrase that now carries the cultural baggage of New Atheism, and which may bring to mind racist, reactionary grifters like Steven Pinker and Richard Dawkins.

2. Jean Charles Léonard de Sismondi (1773–1842) was a liberal Swiss historian and political economist who laid the foundation for many socialist critiques. For example, he wrote the first liberal critique of *laissez-faire* economics, advocated for certain rights for workers—like unemployment, pensions, paid time off, etc.—and was the first to coin the term *proletariat* to refer to the working class under capitalism.

3. Pierre-Joseph Proudhon (1809–1865) was a French politician, philosopher, and economist who was the first person to declare themselves an anarchist, leading many to dub him the "father of anarchism." He is most famous for the assertion that "property is theft" in his book *What is Property? Or, an Inquiry into the Principle of Right and Government.* He also succinctly described anarchy as "order without power." Initially, Proudhon and Karl Marx were friends who greatly influenced one another, but their relationship eventually soured, and their passionate and public falling out became one of the sources of the schism between anarchists and Marxists in the International Working Men's Association.

4. Constantin Meunier (1831–1905) was a Belgian painter and sculptor. His most important contribution to modern art was his elevating of the proletariat—his work often depicted industrial

workers, dock workers, and miners.

5. Ivan Nikolaevich Kubikov (1877–1944) was a literary critic and historian. He was from a family of craft workers and worked at printing houses when he was young. In 1902, he joined the Russian Social Democratic Labor Party and fell in with the Mensheviks the following year. From 1907–1909, he was the Chairman of the St. Petersburg Union of Printers while also lecturing on Russian literature. Following the Russian Revolution of 1905, he was repeatedly arrested by the Tsarist government and was exiled twice. In 1909, he started writing literary criticism in a variety of journals. In 1917, he was actively involved with the Menshevik newspaper "Workers' Thought" (*Rabochaia mysl'*), becoming its editor in 1918. Following the October Revolution, Kubikov withdrew from politics and devoted the rest of his life to teaching and writing literary criticism in Moscow.

6. *Our Dawn* (*Nasha zarya*) was a Menshevik monthly journal started in January 1910 in St. Petersburg. Lenin described the journal as being an organ for Menshevik "liquidators" in Russia—liquidationism being the ideological abandonment of the vanguard party's program. Or, as Lenin himself put it in his article "The Liquidation of Liquidationism": "[it] consists ideologically in negation of the revolutionary class struggle of the socialist proletariat in general, and denial of the hegemony of the proletariat in our bourgeois-democratic revolution in particular." The journal was published until 1914, when it was banned by the Tsarist government.

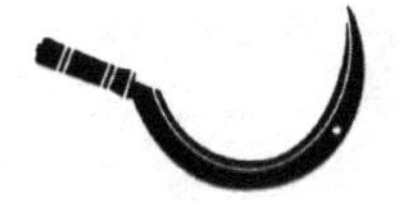

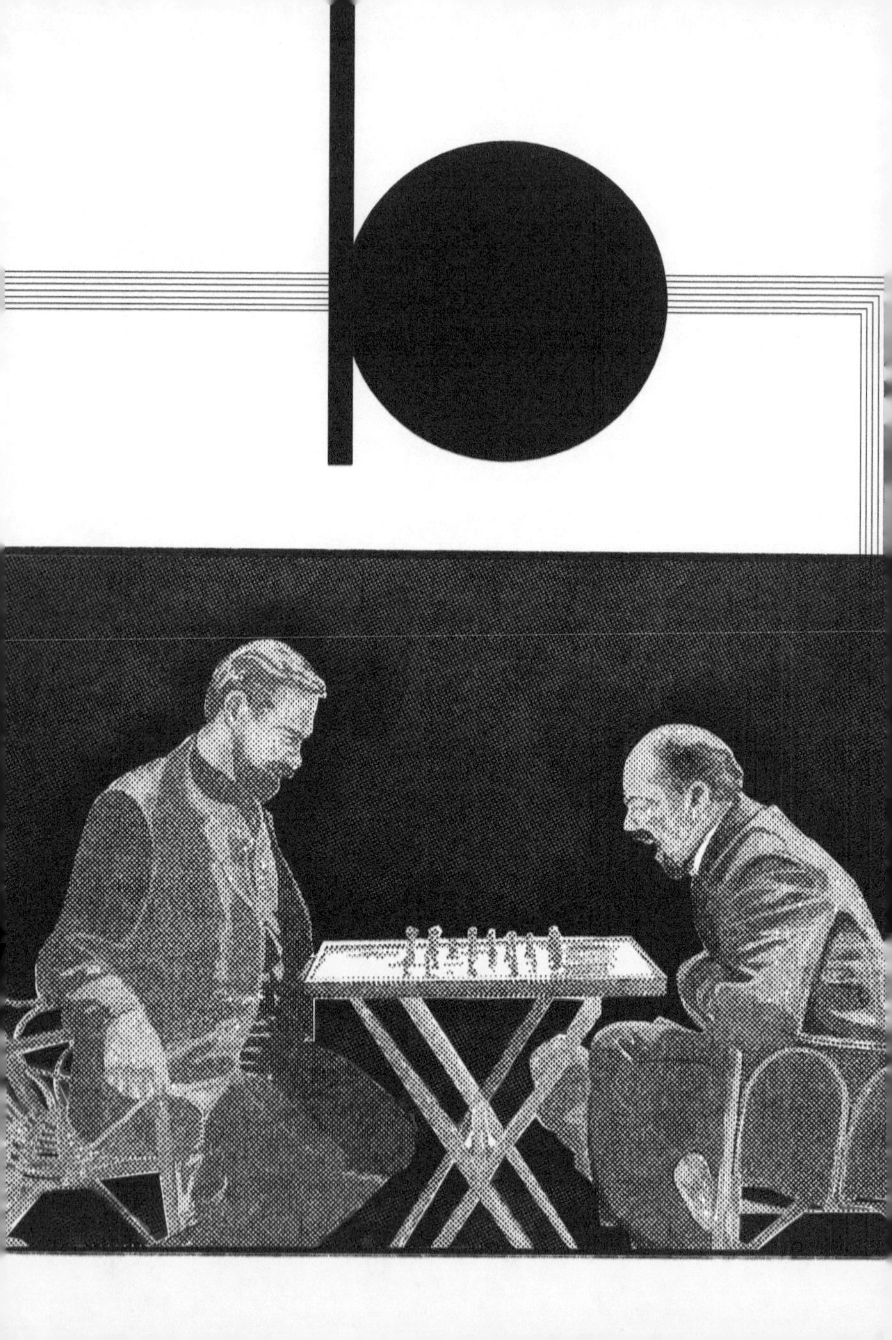

3

# Critique of Proletarian Art

---

Any *creation*—whether natural or human, spontaneous or planned—only leads to an organized, harmonious, viable form through the process of *regulation*. These are two inextricably linked, mutually necessary sides of any *organizational process*. Thus, in the spontaneous development of life, "variability" is a creation; it creates newer combinations of elements—that is to say, newer deviations from older forms. "Natural selection" serves as their regulation: it eliminates forms unsuited to the environment and it preserves and consolidates those that have adapted. In production, the moment of creation is when a labor effort modifies the links between objects; the regulator is a planned control of consciousness which monitors the results of the labor effort, stops it when its immediate goal is reached, redirects it when it deviates from its goal, etc.

In an artist's work, there are the same mechanisms:

new combinations of living images are constantly being created; there too they are regulated by a conscious, planned selection—by a mechanism called "self-criticism"—which sweeps aside everything that is incoherent or does not correspond to the task at hand, and reinforces artistic elements that are proceeding in the right direction. When there is insufficient self-criticism, the result is an incoherent work full of contradictions—a mess of images that falls outside the scope of art.

At a societal level, the development of art is *spontaneously* regulated by the entire social environment, which accepts or rejects the works of art which enter it —which supports or suppresses new artistic trends. But there is also a *planned* regulation: this is called *critique.* Of course, the social environment also contributes to this critique: a work of criticism is carried out from the point of view of any collective and, in a class society, this is from the point of view of this or that class.

Now we will examine by which path, and in which direction, proletarian critique can and should regulate the development of proletarian art.

## I.

The first task of our critique of proletarian art is to establish its boundaries, to clearly define its framework so that it does not become diluted in the surrounding cultural environment—to be sure that it does not mix with the art of the old world. That task is not as simple as it might seem—mistakes and confusion of this type are still constantly observed.

First, one does not usually differentiate proletarian art from peasant art. No doubt the working class, especially our own—the Russian working class— comes from the peasantry and retains points of contact with it: as a mass of people, the peasants are also a working and exploited element of society; it is not for nothing that we could easily create a long-term political alliance with them. But in cooperation and in ideology —in the fundamental means of action and thought— there are deep, fundamental differences *of principle*. The soul of the proletariat—its organizational principle—is centered on collectivism and comradely cooperation; and the more that they develop as a social class, the more this principle develops—the more it penetrates and permeates their lives. As a mass, the peasants and small employers gravitate toward individualism, toward the spirit of private interest and private property—in a word, they are the "petite-bourgeoisie." This name is stereotypical and a bit imprecise because "bourgeois" basically means city-dweller, but it faithfully expresses the basic character of the peasantry's aspirations in life. Additionally, the patriarchal structure of their family maintains the spirit of authoritarianism and religiosity; and in general, this is also facilitated by the inevitable narrowness of their outlook while living in the countryside, and their dependence on a backward agricultural system in which the elements of nature—which are mysterious to the peasant—determines whether or not their fields will yield crops.

Just take a look at peasant poetry. And I am not talking about pre-revolutionary poetry, but current poetry, like that of the Left Socialist-Revolutionaries[1] —although *The Red Call* [*Krasnyy zvon*] is a collection with talented poets such as Klyuev,[2] Yesenin,[3] and others. Despite this, all these poems contain a fetishism of "land," the basis of *their own economy*. Also present are the whole pantheon of peasant gods: the Holy Trinity, the Blessed Virgin, Yegor the Brave,[4] and Nikola the Merciful;[5] and then, there is a constant penchant for the past, an exaltation of leaders who led unorganized and spontaneous uprisings—people such as Stenka Razin[6] ...All of this could not be more foreign to the consciousness of the socialist proletariat.

And yet, such writing is published in workers'

newspapers and magazines as proletarian works and are analyzed by critics under the same designation. It is true that many worker-poets started out by writing peasant poetry, either because they had just recently left their villages and retained a connection with them or simply due to imitation. In this sense, the first publication by worker-poets—released five years ago in Moscow and destroyed by the censors—called *Our Songs* [*Nashi pesni*], Issues I and II, are interesting. A large proportion of these poems are, in fact, purely peasant —but many of them are the more transitional type. It is worth comparing the changing nuances of two or three poems by the same author. Here is V. Torskii, a very beginner poet.

### THE VILLAGE

Here I stand on a hill in my native land,
And my native village lay under me.
The dear peasants of the *izba*[7] stand in a row
They look at the road from the green bushes.
And in the sky burns the cross of the church,
And the birch forest near the church rustles.
The wildflowers bloom all around,
The meadow is belted by a blue ribbon, the river...
The round clouds tighten the sky,
And the sunset appears as an overflowing outfit.

Of course, this is both imitative and weak; but, most importantly, there is not a single line here that would come from a true proletarian poet. Meanwhile, the author's background is actually proletarian; his personal history is far from the peasantry, contrary to what one may think after reading the poem.

Here is more from him:

### THE MORNING

Dawn breaks. The east
Fills with gold.
A gentle breeze blows in
Whispering something to the sleeping groves.
And in his green cloak,
Feeling the morning chill
Together with a clear sky
Youth is reborn.
And only the old pine forest
Sighed suspiciously
Back to the crimson river,
Bent scowling over its curls.

This too is not very original, but there is already a hint of the author's new perception of the world. For the author, the forest is a collective which contains different currents within it that regulate the events of nature differently—yet it is not a separate heroic personality, as it is in Koltsov.[8]

**AUTUMN**.

The tops of the pines are already rustling:
"Autumn is near."
And the melancholy birches
Have lowered their branches.
Like in the old days, they do not argue.
And with hidden anxiety,
They sleepily shake their branches.
They no longer argue, they are only the echo
Without hope, without reproach:
"So soon."
In front of them, like visions,
They quietly fade away into the distance.
Experienced moments
Bright colorful spring.
Caresses from the sun, tales from the wind
Fragrant headwear
Of flowers and fragrant herbs,
A loud chorus of birds,
Intoxicating dreams.
And tears are dripping from the branches
Birch trees, with their white trunks
With a hidden dream in their heart
Without kissing each other,
Without embracing, without admiring
Gilded leaves
A dying dream
Fly quickly into the golden past.

This is the state of mind of the reactionary period; but nature is perceived through the eyes of the collectivist. Its symbols are the general experiences of the forest and not the individual experiences of some birch or pine, as in usual lyrical poetry. Truthful symbols speak of the weakening of collective ties when placed into a situation which suffocates it; the way in which its living links, abandoning themselves to the memories of dreams, withdrawing into themselves, begin to move away from each other. These things do not interest the individualist poet, and therefore, they do not enter their field of vision. Of course, the collectivist way of perceiving and understanding nature —such as here with Torskii—is only one part: it is only one aspect of a complete, real, active collectivism of labor.

Another source of confusion is the military influences that the proletariat was subjected to during the times of war and revolution. The army is basically made up of these same peasants, but they are torn from production, living under the conditions of consumer communism[9] and they are learning, or already practicing, the art of destruction. Their desire for peace, and their hostility toward the rich, momentarily linked soldiers into a political bloc with the proletariat, and created a close relationship between the two— although, as social types, they are not related to each other at all; in fact, they are rather opposed in their roles in life. The consequence of this military comradeship has been that a military tendency has crept into the workers' newspapers and has even painted over the conscience of less principled proletarian poets. Because of this, a specifically military tincture permeated revolutionary themes, thereby violating the noble tone which the class with higher ideals had held. Hence, we saw the importation into poetry of a spirit of narrow-minded, personally-directed hatred toward individual representatives of the bourgeoisie—a spirit understandable in life, but unacceptable in art—this being a feeling that completely distorts the idea of how a great class should be waging our struggle. Likewise, we began seeing outright excesses, in a kind of malevolent mockery of defeated enemies—from a praise of lynching to sadistic delight in the theme of pulling out the intestines of the bourgeoisie. Of course, such things have nothing to do with the ideology of the working class. Working class ideology has its own militant themes, such as an unyielding hatred against capital as a social force; but not petty anger or crude-militarist motives against its individual representatives, who are the inevitable product of their social environment. The proletariat must, of course, take up arms when the interests of its freedom, of its future, and of its ideals demand it; but it should not give in unnecessarily to this kind of societal spontaneity, which is engendered in any armed struggle. The brutality that such a form of struggle arouses in the human soul can, of course, momentarily seize the psyche of combatants, but it is alien and hostile to proletarian culture, which only carries out forced severity. The spirit of genuine strength is moral nobility, and this genuine strength lies in the collectivity of workers. It must become the new aristocracy of culture—the last in the history of humanity, and the first worthy of the name.

Our critique must draw yet another boundary line for proletarian art—this time on the side of intellectual socialism. There, confusion is very natural and particularly understandable because the intelligentsia and artistic movements are so close to one another. But the differences are still deep and important.

The working intelligentsia emerged from bourgeois culture. They were brought up on bourgeois culture and they worked on, and for, bourgeois culture. Its principles rest on the individualism of the scientist, artist, or writer. Collaboration is never felt directly— the role of the collective remains out of sight, the superficial appearance of isolation is dominant, and there is the illusion of completely independent personal activity. The very nature of intellectual labor supports these tendencies. When there is obvious collaboration, then the intellectual usually occupies the authoritarian position of a leader, of an organizer of work: an engineer in a factory, a doctor in a hospital, etc. And from this comes the element of authoritarianism which inevitably persists in the bourgeois world and its culture —as an organizational addition to their otherwise fundamental anarchy.

Because of all this, even though the intellectual worker has a sincere and deep sympathy for the working class, and has faith in the socialist ideal, the past retains its strength in their way of thinking, in their perception of life, and in their understanding of the forces and paths of their development.

An example is Verhaeren's drama *The Dawn*.[10] We not only reference it immediately when it comes to the repertoire of the proletarian theatre, but we even consider it possible to stage the drama without any interpretation or commentary—as if it were entirely "our own." This is a mistake. The play is beautiful and is, for us, a precious piece of our heritage; but nevertheless, it is a piece of heritage from the old world. In it, the spirit of socialism is enveloped in authoritarian and individualistic garb, which must be understood, and which is impossible to simply accept. Everything is built upon the heroic personality of a popular tribune of the people leading the masses; they are the soul of the struggle and of victory—without them the masses are ignorant and blind, unable to find their way. For the author, the tragedy of this character constitutes the principal interest of the entire play. This is how the old world understands the meaning of personality. Collectivism constructs life differently and enlightens it differently. Collectivism, of course, recognizes heroes; but more importantly, it creates them—and it creates them as the embodiment of the strength of the *collective*, as the spokesperson of *its* common will, as the interpreter of *its* ideal.

Therefore, as long as social relations with our heroes remain at odds with the above criteria, this means the proletarian collective has not yet matured into a clear consciousness of itself.

In his statues, which express the everyday lives of workers, the great Belgian sculptor Constantin Meunier produced a real cult of *labor*. Yet despite all the depth of the artist's love for those he depicted—with all his sympathetic understanding—it was not yet a cult of the *collective*. His talent remains enormous; however, the proletarian artist must know that for them, this is not a ready-made guide—their tasks go much further.

The artistic consciousness of the working class must be pure and clear, free from extraneous additions: this is the primary concern of our critique.

## II.

Our critique of proletarian art should, first and foremost, focus on its content.

The nascent art of a young class—which, moreover, lives in difficult conditions—is inevitably characterized by a certain *narrowness* of content. It stems from a lack of experience, from the obligatory mediocrity of its field of observation. Therefore, fiction, at first, begins by reluctantly taking all its themes and material from the everyday life of the workers themselves, or even from that of the revolutionary intellectuals associated with them; until now, it is only little by little that they have widened their domain. However, it is indisputable that proletarian art must capture, in the field of its experience, all of society and nature—all of the life of the universe.

What can our critique do in this respect? Of course, it is unable to immediately give young art what it lacks. But it can, and must, constantly challenge the expansion of the field; it can, and must, indicate new possibilities. And it will bring indirect but very real aid to this progress by comparing—as soon as it has the opportunity—the works of proletarian art with the works of old art, especially where proletarian and old art each share a similar "artistic idea." In that space of comparison, the material, the field of view, and often the very principles of solving artistic problems will turn out to be different.

This relates particularly to the favored questions of classical literature: about the structure of the family, the struggle between "lower" and "higher" motivations of the human soul, the dominant passion that motivates a person, the education of character, etc.

In one way or another, we have often posed the same, or similar, tasks that have already been resolved by science and philosophy. It is up to critique to point out that alongside these resolutions, there are also worthy artistic comparisons: the great collectivism of the pan-human experience—which the world of science conceals—will, in most cases, be a precious guide for younger comrades who are seeking to stabilize their wavering creativity.

The narrowness of their artistic content is not only due to a limited consideration of organizable experiences, but it is also due to a narrowed, one-sided perception—to a limited basic attitude toward the material of the experience. Typical examples of this include the excessive concentration on the point of view of social struggle and the reduction of art to an *organizing-combative* role. This narrowing of content is quite natural for a young and struggling class, particularly in the most difficult of situations; it is even necessary at the first stages of class development, when content becomes self-determined through the consciousness of its opposition to another class in society, and therefore it concentrates mostly on developing the fighting side of its ideology. But then, just as inevitably, this point of view becomes insufficient.

It is through struggle that the working class advances towards its ideal; this ideal is not destruction, but instead a new organization of life. It is an extraordinarily new form of life, immeasurably complex, and supremely harmonious. Consequently, the cultivation of a militant consciousness is not, in itself, the primary means of accomplishing this task; it is necessary to develop a socially constructive ideology. Proletarian science is already moving in this direction, and proletarian art must follow with even more energy and speed—particularly as the working class begins to approach the realization of its ideal.

In present-day proletarian poetry, the poetry of agitation is predominant, particularly in our country. All other poetry drowns amid the thousands of poems which call for the class struggle and which glorify its victories; they drown amid hundreds of stories denouncing capital and its servants. This must change. The part does not have to be the whole. It is true that a comprehensive dive into life is more difficult than writing about breaking through an enemy line, but the former is even more necessary in the cause for socialism because it is only with a comprehensive understanding of life and its concrete forces which will give support to a pervasive, practical, and universal creativity.

The reduction of poetry to solely civic agitation adversely affects its very artistry, which is essential to its organizing force. The dominance of the cliché is developing: how is originality preserved after thousands of repetitions? The sympathy which unites the masses with the poet will begin to dull.

And then, although the content will have progressed, it is often still understood according to an older point of view, which is narrower than it needs to be. For example, the central theme of A.K. Gastev's recent book is the enormous organizing power of mechanized production—that is, the inherent connections within it that unite the labor collective, as well as its inherent power, including the machine's power over the elements. This is one of the basic ideas of a *cultural-creative* proletarian consciousness; but Gastev titled his book *Poetry of the Worker's Blow*, as if the task did not go beyond the limits of the *fighting* consciousness of the proletariat. Moreover, it is obvious that the expression of a "worker's blow"—

particularly within a time of violent revolution—evokes in everyone the idea of a social battle, and not at all the idea of the strike of a hammer, which, as an aside, is an insufficient symbol for mechanized technology anyway.

The agitational narrowing of artistic ideas is also portrayed in such tones as if the capitalists, and the bourgeois intellectuals who support them, were *personally* evil, cruel, dishonest, etc. Such an understanding is naïve and contradicts the collectivist method of thinking. It is not at all a matter of the personal characteristics of this or that member of the bourgeoisie which are in question, and it is not against isolated individuals that the revolutionary effort should be directed. What we are against are the class positions of these individuals; and we wage our struggle against the social system and against the collectives associated with it, as well as those who are defending it. The capitalist may otherwise be a most distinguished individual personally, but since they are a member of their class, their actions and thoughts will necessarily be determined by their social position. Even at the moment of a military clash, to a class-conscious proletarian, they are an enemy not as an individual, but as a blind link in a chain forged by history. To defeat the old world, it is more useful to understand it as being made up of its best representatives in their highest manifestations than to imagine that it is made up of only evil people with bad motives. The collective thinking and will of the working class must not be exchanged for such trivial minutiae.

Closely related to the same agitational narrowing of creativity is a recent theory that demands that proletarian art must always be "sparking with life" and enthusiastic. Although this cannot be described as anything other than childish, it has unfortunately found an undeniable success, especially among the younger and less experienced proletarian poets. The range of feelings in the working class cannot, and should not, be so limited. Undoubtedly, the labor collective is characterized by an acute and vivid sense of its own strength; but we must not forget that strength itself sometimes suffers defeats. Above all, art must be sincere and truthful, especially in its role as an organizer of life: if an artist is not to be trusted, then who can they organize?

In May of this year, the following verses could be read in a workers' newspaper:

> I am walking in the radiance of the sun and spring...
> The horizon burns with scarlet flowers.
> Unrealizable dreams have come true,
> And souls are lifted to great heights,
> Like the mighty peaks of mountains.

What days! What horizons!
Through the fields, through the winding streams,
By the crystal dawns, and evening dreams,
By the loud, booming trains,
By the smiles on their faces, and the garlands of words—
Like beads in the petals of crimson flowers,
Joy sparkles in our days.
To the bottom, to the bosom of their depths
I am drunk with crimson joy, drunk with the sun
...etc.

In our country, the "unrealizable dreams" which really "came true" in those days were the "scarlet" dreams of the German imperialists, which the proletariat did not have the strength to repel. Those were the days of heavy hardships and frequent anguish during our revolution; days of fierce abuse directed at our comrades in Ukraine, the Caucasus, Finland, the Baltic States; days of painful weariness in the face of the enormous, overwhelming tasks of our country; days of disarray and hunger; days of the rise of all we have inherited from that cursed war... Yes, despair is unworthy of fighters—but the falsehood of rose-tinted glasses is even worse: it is a retreat, an escape from reality, a false mask of this same despair...

This reduces proletarian poetry to the level of those whose motto is:

The exhilarating lie
Is dearer to us than low truths in the darkness.


No, we do not want sweet words, but unyielding will and historical pride—this is what the proletariat needs when surrounded by enemies from all sides:


*Si fractus illabatur orbis,*
*Impavidum ferient ruinae—*[11]


"If the world should break and fall about them, its ruins would strike them fearless." This ancient poet-individualist knew what true courage was. The poet of our new collective should not be outdone.

In all its regulatory work, our critique of proletarian creativity must always keep one thing in mind: *the spirit of labor collectivism is, above all, objectivity.*


# III.

The critique of proletarian art which focuses on its *form* must pursue one well-defined and very clear task: *the complete harmony between form and content.*

The proletariat must, of course, begin by learning artistic techniques from its predecessors. In doing so, there is a natural temptation to take as an example the most recent developments which have been worked out by older art movements. While doing this, however, it is easy to make mistakes.

In art, form is inextricably linked to content, and whatever movement happens to be the most recent is not always the most perfect. When a social class has fulfilled its progressive role within the historical process, and it begins its decline, then the content of its art inevitably becomes decadent; but this form follows closely behind its content, and it begins to accommodate itself to whatever the emerging style happens to be. The degeneration of a ruling class usually involves a transition to parasitism. This is followed by satiety, which ends up dulling any meaning in life. It is from this dulled meaning of life that new content begins to develop, since creative activity derives from a social point of view; however, this content develops when life becomes deserted, when it loses its "reasonable" meaning—that is to say, precisely, when it loses its social meaning. We try to fill this void by looking for new pleasures or sensations. Art organizes these searches—on the one hand, by arousing a fading sensuality, it sets off in the direction of decadent perversions; on the other hand, by refining and sharpening aesthetic perceptions, it begins to overcomplicate matters, and its form becomes adorned with petty gimmicks. There are many historical examples of this during the decline of various cultures: byzantine, ancient, and feudal cultures—and, in recent decades, due to the disintegration of bourgeois culture, this includes most currents in the decadent "modernism" and "futurism" movements. Russian bourgeois art is modeled upon European bourgeois art and—much like our bourgeoisie itself, being both cachectic and flabby—is fading away without having experienced any real flourishing.

In general, and for the most part, one should not learn artistic techniques from these organizers of a decaying life, but instead from the great works of art generated by the rise and flourishing of the now obsolete classes, ranging from revolutionary romantics to classical artists from different eras. From the most recent currents, one can only learn gimmicks, even though, it is true, they are often produced by great masters; but this knowledge must be acquired with caution and circumspection so that as one learns from these styles, they do not pick up the germs of decay from which they came.

It is distressing to see when a poet-proletarian is looking for the best artistic forms and they think they will find them in some show-off intellectual advertiser like Mayakovsky[12]—or even worse, in someone like

Igor Severyanin,[13] the ideologue of gigolos and courtesans, a talented embodiment of lacquered vulgarity. We have had great masters who are worthy of being the first teachers of art forms to the great class, but they are not these men.

The simplicity, clarity, and purity of artistic form present in the great Russian masters—Pushkin, Lermontov, Gogol, Nekrasov, Tolstoy—respond better than anything else to the tasks of emerging art. Of course, new content inevitably develops new forms; but we must proceed from the best which has already existed. As for recent forms, it is necessary to study those who are mutually coherent and artistically stable, and not those who are distant and changing—not those who come and go, like the Andreyevs, the Balmonts, the Bloks, etc.[14]

Our working poetry, from the beginning, has shown a penchant for rhythmic verses and simple rhymes. Now it shows much more of an inclination toward free rhythms and intricately intertwined verses with new, complex, and often unexpected rhymes. The influence of the latest intellectual poetry is clearly felt here, and it should hardly be welcomed. The new forms are far more difficult; to fight against them, though, is an unnecessary expenditure of energy which would distract from the most important thing: the elaboration and the development of artistic content.

Let there be some uniformity in what is right; this follows from life itself. The factory worker lives in the realm of strict rhythms and simple, elementary rhymes. Amid their "chaos of steel"—moving looms and machines intertwine in waves of different, but mechanically precise rhythms; at the same time, the continuity of smaller and more frequent rhythms are traversed by less frequent and heavier rhythms, much like caesura or rhyme in verse. These sounds, with their endlessly repeating strokes and blows, forge verbal images in their own measure, to which a worker with a creative nature will try to artistically match with their own experience.

Consequently, when the rhythms of living nature become accessible to the worker—when there is the least amount of mechanical repetition and regularity—this monotony will disappear by itself. But overcoming it by imitating poets from foreign backgrounds and situations is an unnecessary task that only perpetuates difficulties—and difficulties are already plentiful. It is no coincidence that Samobytnik, the best poet-worker so far, did not follow this path.

The most difficult form for young poetry is prose poetry. Rejecting the rhyme and obvious rhythm of sounds, it requires on one hand a more harmonious rhythm of imagery, and on the other hand a sufficient harmony of sound combinations. These requirements are far from being completely mastered in A.K. Gastev's work *Poetry of the Worker's Blow*, where prose poetry predominates. Here we can see the inexperience of young creativity; he is carried away on a path that is still too difficult—although perhaps it is simply out of ignorance of the difficulties of this form. Our critique can save a great deal of artistic effort by clarifying the hidden complications inherent in various forms—an issue which the old theory of art had little interest in doing.

A living example of why it is necessary for new art workers to have a foundational knowledge in art theory can be seen in the misunderstandings surrounding the publishing of Bessalko's[15] work *Catastrophe*. The book is called a "novel," when in reality, it is a large story. The difference between these two forms is quite vague in the usual theories of literature, but our critique allows us to figure out these differences relatively easily and accurately. In a story, the posing of organizational problems and their solutions is *episodic*; in this case, the author wanted to show how a compositionally mixed revolutionary collective becomes disorganized in an atmosphere of extreme oppression, where it is impossible to act. If the author had posed and solved the problem in a *systemic* way, he would have clarified the origin and the development of the various elements that composed of the revolutionary collective, the conditions which temporarily banded them together, and the objective necessity of decomposition and disintegration—and it is in this latter technique, not the former, that would have made it a novel. It is not a matter of length: a novel can be shorter than a long story.

Our critique will create—step by step, through its living practice—a new theory of art in which it will find a place for all the richness of the experiences present within older critique, but it will be re-examined and re-systematized from a higher point of view, namely from a pan-organizational perspective.

It should be noted that, in other cases, the critique of form is absolutely inseparable from the critique of content—and in reality, one often follows the other. This is particularly true for the question of artistic symbols. A symbol is a living image which serves as a special kind of sign for a whole series of other images related to it, as a means of bringing these images together simultaneously—and in an organized manner —into one's consciousness. Thus, the apparition of Hamlet's father is a symbol of the muffled echoes of a criminal affair which is gradually developing in his social environment, and which eventually reveals its secret. The Great City in Verhaeren's *The Dawn* is a symbol of the whole organization of capitalist society. But, as a living image and not as a naked sign, such a symbol has its own content which is, moreover, the first to be perceived. The apparition is a ghost; the Great City is some kind of capital. This very content is subject to all the laws of art and its corresponding critique. If, for example, the ghost of Hamlet's father did not behave as the popular imagination believes ghosts should behave, then it would result in a gross lack of artistic sense. Despite all the depth of his ideas, Maeterlinck's[16] *The Blue Bird* would not have been such a great work if its symbols had not formed into the beautiful, harmonious fairy tale that children like so much.

Our critique, of course, must also tackle symbols from this pragmatic aspect, starting with their very choice.

Our cruel and crude era—the era of militarism in action—often encourages artists to utilize cruel and crude symbols. Suppose, for example, that in order to express—in an especially sharp and clear manner—the idea of rejecting all that is personal in the name of a great collective cause, a worker-writer makes the hero in their story murder a beloved and sympathetic woman. Critics must say that such a symbol is unacceptable: it contradicts the very idea of collectivism. The woman in this example is not a source of personal happiness, but another human being, and a possible member of the same collective. Or, for example, the poet who, wishing to express his determination to fight to the end against the old world without shrinking from any sacrifice—even the most horrible and most difficult threats—may write:

> In the name of our Tomorrow, we will burn the Raphaels,
> We will destroy museums, we will trample on the flowers
> of art.[17]

One comrade reviewer correctly noted (albeit too mildly in my opinion), that this is "psychology, not ideology"; that is, the poet, by abandoning himself to the flow of his *personal* feelings, has forgotten the *social* role of organizing art. This image is a symbol of a soldier's spirit, not that of a worker. The soldier can and should bombard the Reims Cathedral if an enemy observation post is located there, or is supposed to be there; but what makes a poet choose this Hindenburgian[18] image? A poet should only regret such a cruel necessity, and they certainly should not celebrate it. When a poet's creativity is this unmoored, it is unable to be elevated. The proletarian must never forget that, in the present, *collaboration between generations* is the opposite of collaboration between classes. The poet does not have the right to disrespect the great dead who paved the way for us and who bequeathed their souls to us—who, from the grave, extend a helping hand to us in our pursuit of the ideal.

Whether it is the form or the content of art, our critique must constantly remind the artist of their responsibility as the organizer of the living forces for a great collective.

## IV.

Critique works as a regulator of artistic life, not only at the level of its creativity, but also from the level of its perception. It is an *interpreter* of art for the broad masses. It shows people what they can take from art to help them arrange their lives, both internally and externally —and how to do so.

But, compared to the art of the old world, our critique is forced to limit itself to the following: it cannot regulate its own development. But, compared to newer art—that is, our art—both aspects are equally urgent and enormous.

Here it is not only a matter of helping to reveal symbols after years of having them not be understood, or explaining what is hidden in the images which, perhaps, the artist themselves may not be able to accurately formulate—or even to draw all the conclusions which the artist themselves may not have had time to articulate. Critique should indicate both new questions that may arise on the basis of that work's achievement as well as the new possibilities that emanate from it. But the most important thing is that critique must introduce for the masses a new system of work that develops a class culture—that develops a common connection of proletarian world relations in living images, both concrete and particular—that finds and shows the meaning of the world revealed by the pan-organizational point of view.

It is on this path that our critique itself will then turn into creativity.

# NOTES

1. The Party of Socialist Revolutionaries (commonly abbreviated as SRs) was a political party founded at the end of 1901 following the merger of several different populist groups. After the February Revolution in 1917 the SRs played an active role in the Provisional Government, garnering major support from the rural population in Russia. By the summer of 1917, on the eve of the October Revolution, the party split between those who continued to support the Provisional Government (referred to as Right SRs) and those who backed the Bolsheviks (referred to as the Left SRs; this is who Bogdanov is referencing here). After the October Revolution, the Left SRs formed a coalition government with the Bolsheviks but resigned *en masse* following the signing of the Treaty of Brest-Litovsk, which they vehemently opposed. The Left SRs then waged several uprisings against the Bolshevik government (mostly in Moscow and Yaroslavl) and even succeeded in assassinating the German ambassador, Count Wilhelm von Mirbach on July 6, 1918. Following this brief rebellion, most of the Left SRs were arrested. That said, there were many Left SRs that opposed the uprising and formed small pro-Bolshevik parties, continuing to serve in the government and bureaucracy. By 1921, as the Civil War was winding down, all the pro-Bolshevik Left SR splinter groups merged with the All-Russian Communist Party (Bolsheviks), which then became the Communist Party of the Soviet Union.

2. Nikolai Alekseevich Klyuev (1884–1937) was a symbolist poet and one of the first of the "peasant poets." He loved Russian folklore and his poetry focused on the beauty of peasant life. He was also openly gay, with homoeroticism playing a part in many of his poems. He was a close friend and mentor to the lyrical Imaginist poet Sergei Yesenin (see endnote 3). He was arrested in

1933 on charges of "contradicting Soviet ideology" by allegedly supporting the *kulaks*. He was either shot or died in a labor camp in 1937.

3. Sergei Alexandrovich Yesenin (1895–1925) was a lyrical poet who helped found the post-revolutionary, avant-garde poetic movement called Imaginism. His poems centered on nostalgia for the village life of his childhood and often shunned urbanization and industrialization. He also wrote many revolutionary poems throughout 1917–1919 and became a member of the All-Russian Union of Poets. He married four times throughout his life; his third wife being the American dancer Isadora Duncan, whom he traveled throughout Europe and the United States with in 1922–1923. In his autobiography he wrote "I dislike America intensely. America is a stinking place where not just art is being murdered, but with it, all the loftiest aspirations of humankind..." Following his trip to the U.S. (and another subsequent divorce and re-marrying), he began to exhibit signs of depression and alcoholism. In the beginning of 1924, he was arrested and interrogated four times for drunkenness and public outbursts. On December 28, 1925, he was found dead by suicide in his room in the Hotel Angleterre in Leningrad. The day before, he had written his final poem "Goodbye, my friend, goodbye" (*Do svidan'ya, drug moy, do svidan'ya*) in his own blood.

4. Yegor the Brave (also known as Yuri or George) is a reference to the Orthodox Christian Saint George, of which the pastoralist George's Day is celebrated as the day of the first cattle drive to pasture and a day of the ritual milking of sheep.

5. Nikola the Merciful is a reference to the Orthodox Christian Saint Nicholas the Merciful, who is said to have performed miracles as numerous as the stars of heaven.

6. Stepan Timofeyevich Razin (1630–1671), known as Stenka

Razin, was a Cossack who led a rebellion against the Tsar in 1670–1671. His uprising was a reaction following the so-called Time of Troubles (*Smutnoe vremya*) which lasted from the death of the last male line of the Rurik dynasty in 1598 until the Romanov dynasty took power in 1613. During that 15-year period, many of the peasants, including the autonomously minded Cossacks, were essentially able to practice unmediated self-governance due to the royal power vacuum. However, after the ascension of the Romanovs, a strong, centralized autocracy began to take hold and the peasants rebelled under Stenka Razin's leadership. The rebels pillaged villages in the hopes of taking power from government officials and restoring greater autonomy to the peasants. Razin was captured in 1671 by Cossack elders and handed over to the Tsar. On June 6, 1671, he was quartered on a scaffold in Moscow's Red Square.

7. *Izba*, also called *khata*, is a traditional log house often found on Russian farmsteads and in rural areas.

8. Here Bogdanov is most likely referring to Aleksey Vasilievich Koltsov (1809–1842), a poet and collector of Russian folklore. His poetry celebrated the work and lives of simple peasants—with a focus on his romantic and idealized ideas of what agricultural labor was like.

9. This is a term that Bogdanov used to describe War Communism, which—following his analysis of World War I—he argued was a necessary period used by most industrialized countries during times of war; the suspension of traditional capitalist relations for more collectivist principles allowed for a smooth funneling of goods, materiel, and personnel into a country's war machine. However, as he argues in this paragraph, he believed that when the bulk of a ruling political party is made up of soldiers, their inherent militaristic culture permeates—and subsequently narrows—what it sees are its social possibilities. He also believed that War

Communism had the potential to degrade into state capitalism.

10. The Belgian poet and art critic Émile Adolphe Gustave Verhaeren (1855–1916) was, at that time, very fashionable in Russian revolutionary circles. He was one of the founders of the Symbolism school of art and was nominated six times for the Nobel Prize in Literature. His play *The Dawn* was especially popular; the show was famously staged in 1921 by the experimental Soviet theatre director, actor, and producer Vsevolod Meyerhold (1874–1940).

11. This is a quote from the Roman lyrical poet Quintus Horatius Flaccus (65 BCE–27 BCE), more commonly known as Horace. This verse is from his work entitled *Odes*.

12. Vladimir Vladimirovich Mayakovsky (1893–1930) was a Soviet poet, playwright, artist, and actor. Prior to the Revolution, he was a prominent figure in the Russian Futurist movement, co-signing the Futurist manifesto *A Slap in the Face of Public Taste* (*Poshchochina obshchestvennomu vkusu*) in 1913. He produced an enormous and diverse body of work throughout his relatively short career including poetry, directing (and authoring) plays, acting in films, editing art journals, and producing an abundance of agitprop in support of the Communist Party, especially during the Civil War years. Although his work regularly praised the Bolsheviks—and he produced many pieces of agitprop in praise of Lenin, which is perhaps why Bogdanov is so prickly with him here—he also clashed with the Soviet state over cultural censorship, and he resisted the development of Socialist Realism. On April 12, 1930, he committed suicide by shooting himself through the heart. On April 17, 1930, his funeral was attended by an estimated 150,000 people—the third largest public event of mourning in Soviet history, only surpassed by the funerals of Lenin and Stalin.

13. Igor Vasilyevich Severyanin (1887–1941) was a poet who was

the most prominent member of the literary group called the Ego-Futurists, who significantly influenced the Imaginists in the 1920s. Severyanin was known to be incredibly egotistical, vulgar, and would often shock his bourgeois audience by making cynical or megalomaniacal statements. After the Russian Revolution, he left Russia for Estonia, where he settled for the remainder of his life. He died in Nazi-occupied Tallinn in 1941.

14. Here Bogdanov is referencing several artists involved in the Russian Symbolist movement. He's referring specifically to Leonid Nikolaievich Andreyev (1871–1919), Konstantin Dmitriyevich Balmont (1867–1942), and Alexander Alexandrovich Blok (1880–1921).

15. Pavel Karpovich Bessalko (1887–1920) was a proletarian prose poet and revolutionary. He grew up a peasant and had virtually no formal education, but he was recognized as a poet of natural talent by, among others, Anatoly Lunacharsky and Bogdanov. In 1903, he joined the Russian Social Democratic Labor Party and affiliated himself with the Menshevik faction. In 1907, he was arrested for revolutionary activity, imprisoned for two years, and then exiled. Bessalko managed to escape exile and lived abroad in France from 1910–1917, working as a fitter for a French aircraft factory and writing in his spare time. When news of the October Revolution reached him, he immediately returned to Russia and joined the Bolsheviks, working as a journalist. He was active in the Petrograd Proletkult with Bogdanov and wrote for their journal *The Future* (*Gryadushcheye*). In 1919, during the Civil War, he was mobilized and sent to the Ukrainian front, where he edited a Red Army newspaper. He died of typhus in Kharkov in the autumn of 1920.

16. Maurice Polydore Marie Bernard Maeterlinck (1862–1949) was a Belgian playwright, poet, and essayist. He won the Nobel Prize in Literature in 1911 and was made a Count in 1932. His plays formed an important part of the Symbolist movement in Russia.

His play *The Blue Bird*, referenced above, premiered on September 30, 1908, at Konstantin Stanislavski's Moscow Art Theatre. It was also staged on Broadway in 1910.

17. This is a famous quote by the previously cited Vladimir Kirillov. It is from his poem "We" (*My*) which was published in 1918 in the journal *Proletarian Culture* (*Proletarskaya kul'tura*), which, incidentally, published the chapters of this book as separate articles in the same year.

18. Bogdanov is referencing the bombardment of the Reims Cathedral by the Imperial German Army during World War I, then under the command of Paul von Hindenburg. The famed zeppelin airship that was named after him did not exist yet and it would not face its fiery demise for another 19 years, in 1937.

# BIBLIOGRAPHY


Bogdanov, Alexander. "Iz psikhologii obshchestva." St. Petersburg, 1906.

———. *Red Star: The First Bolshevik Utopia.* Edited by Loren R. Graham and Richard Stites. Translated by Charles Rougle. Indiana University Press, 1984.

———. "Kul'turnye zadachi nashego vremeni." Moscow, 1911.

———. "Sud'by rabochey partii v nyneshney revolyutsii." *Novaya zhizn'* 19–20, 1918a.

———. "Voprosy sotsializma." Moscow, 1918b.

———. "Elementy proletarskoy kul'tury v razvitii rabochego klassa." Moscow, 1920.

———. *The Philosophy of Living Experience.* Translated, edited, and introduced by David G. Rowley. Haymarket Books, 2016.

Genovese, Taylor R. "How the egalitarian dreams that fueled the quest for 'young blood' treatments got perverted." *The Washington Post*, March 27, 2019.

Gramsci, Antonio. *Selections from the Prison Notebooks.* International Publishers, 1971.

Joravsky, David. "The Construction of the Stalinist Psyche." In *Cultural Revolution in Russia*, 1928–1931, edited by Sheila Fitzpatrick, Indiana University Press, 105–128, 1978.

Krementsov, Nikolai. *A Martian Stranded on Earth: Alexander Bogdanov, Blood Transfusions, and Proletarian Science*. University of Chicago Press, 2011.

Lenin, V.I. "What Is to Be Done? Burning Questions of Our Movement." In *V.I. Lenin Collected Works Volume 5*. Progress Publishers, 347–529, 1960.

———. "The Liquidation of Liquidationism." In *V.I. Lenin Collected Works Volume 15*. Progress Publishers, 452–460, 1963.

———. "Speech at the First Congress of Economic Councils, May 26, 1918." In *V.I. Lenin Collected Works Volume 27*. Progress Publishers, 408–415, 1965.

———. "Our Foreign and Domestic Position and The Tasks of The Party: Speech Delivered to the Moscow Gubernia Conference of the R.C.P.(B.), November 21, 1920." In *V.I. Lenin Collected Works Volume 31*. Progress Publishers, 408–426, 1966.

Scherrer, Jutta. "The Relationship between the Intelligentsia and Workers: The Case of the Party Schools in Capri and Bologna." In *Workers and Intelligentsia in Late Imperial Russia: Realities, Representations, Reflections*, edited by Reginald E. Zelnik, University of California, Berkeley, 172–185, 1998.

Sochor, Zenovia A. *Revolution and Culture: The Bogdanov-Lenin Controversy*. Cornell University Press, 1988.

Utechin, S.V. "Bolsheviks and Their Allies after 1917: The Ideological Pattern." *Soviet Studies* 10 (2): 113–135, 1958.

Velminski, Wladimir. *Homo Sovieticus: Brain Waves, Mind Control, and Telepathic Destiny*, MIT Press, 2017.

White, James D. *Red Hamlet: The Life and Ideas of Alexander Bogdanov.* Haymarket Books, 2019.

Williams, Robert C. "Collective Immortality: The Syndicalist Origins of Proletarian Culture, 1905–1910." *Slavic Review* 39 (3), 389–402, 1980.

Zalkind, Aron B. "O zabolevaniiakh partaktiva." *Krasnaya Nov'* 4: 187–203, 1925.

Zetkin, Klara. *My Recollections of Lenin.* Foreign Languages Publishing House, 1956.